BIRM
Univer

an Anthology

Edited by
Helena Hoar, Shirley Lloyd, Joel Rawlin,
Shauntelle Trotter, and Dan Witherall

Editorial Consultant: **Alan Mahar**

Published by **Imprimata**
for and on behalf of The School of English, Birmingham City University.

First published 2016
Compilation © The School of English,
Birmingham City University 2016
Contributions © individual copyright holders

The School of English, Birmingham City University has asserted its
rights under the Copyright Designs and Patents Act 1988
to be identified as the author of this compilation.
All rights reserved. No part of this publication may be reproduced,
stored in or introduced into a retrieval system, or transmitted in any
form or by any means, (electronic, mechanical, photocopying, recording
or otherwise, and whether invented now or subsequently) without the
prior written permission of The School of English, Birmingham City
University, or be otherwise circulated in any form, other than that in
which it is published, without a similar condition being imposed
on any subsequent publisher.
Any person who does any unauthorized act in relation to this
publication may be liable to criminal prosecution and civil action.

A CIP Catalogue record for this book is available
from the British library

ISBN 978-1-906192-92-1

Cover image, design and
typesetting by Mark Bracey

Printed in Great Britain
InX-192921-16

An imprint of InXmedia Limited
Trident Court, 1 Oakcroft Road, Chessington, Surrey KT9 1BD, UK

Contents

Foreword		v
Chuck Newsey	*The Tamale Guy*	1
Ted Bonham	*Call for Contributions*	7
Nicholas Doran	*The Happiest World on Earth*	9
Helena Hoar	*The Cradley Tragedy*	18
Olivia Hodgson	*The Mechanic*	21
Olivia Hodgson	*Digbeth*	22
Rhoda Greaves	*Sunday Roast*	23
Richard Hughes	*The Passion of Dr Abacus*	24
Joe Legge	*Bethany*	37
Jack Warren	*All my mates have become clowns*	41
Jack Warren	*Self-portrait as Digbeth Branch canal*	42
Jack Warren	*Preparing for spring*	43
Dan Witherall	*Release*	44
Jan Barker	*At the Edge of my Mind*	56
Joel Rawlin	*The Girl from Work*	60
Jim Crace	1, from *The Devil's Larder*	61
Jim Crace	2, from *The Devil's Larder*	63
Gregory Leadbetter	*Imp*	65
Gregory Leadbetter	*Stalking*	67
Siren Knight	*Noir*	68
Shirley Lloyd	*Pause*	73
Tony Howe	*Arle*	75
Jack Roberts	*Spectrum*	76
Richard Hughes	*Summer Vegetables*	81

Nicholas Doran	*Enker Green*	83
Siren Knight	*Arm's Length*	90
Joe Legge	*Tarrare*	92
Derek Littlewood	*Trans-Siberian Journey*	98
Joel Rawlin	*Whispers*	100
Anna Lawrence Pietroni	*'Night thickened and from the north, snowflakes'*	108
David Roberts	*The Petition*	109
Derek Littlewood	*The Secret Languages of Ireland*	114
Rhoda Greaves	*Her Body*	116
Notes on the Contributors		117

Foreword

Students at Birmingham City University who have aspirations to write for a living or just for pleasure are immensely fortunate these days. There are creative writing classes, there are hands-on encounters with writers and the writing life, there are members of staff ready to mentor the manuscripts whether they be fiction, poetry, drama or journalism, there is a culture of support for the creative talents as well as for the academic, there is, indeed, this anthology of new work which offers a first experience of publishing to anyone with ability and ambition.

In my day, during the mid-1960s as a student of English Literature at the Birmingham College of Commerce (one of the early component parts of BCU) we were trained to be discerning readers but actual authors, living or dead, were regarded as a separate exotic species to be appreciated from a distance. There was no more expectation that we could become writers ourselves than that natural history students might turn into frogs.

As it happens and despite the woeful lack of any encouragement, there were -other than myself- at least three published novelists who were my contemporaries at the College of Commerce, John Wheway, Gordon Burn, and Patrick McGrath. Old school purists might argue that such successes are evidence that "talent will out" and that writers have no need for formal instruction or guidance. Creative writing can't be taught, in other words. Well, possibly it's true that genius is just the gift of fortune, but skill is not, and nor is opportunity. Great musicians, no matter how innately talented they are, are unlikely to have much success without access to instruments or without early tuition or without attention to their scales or chords. So it is with writers too. At BCU, talent teams up with instruction and with encouragement to produce written works of considerable originality and achievement.

The pages that follow are my evidence.

Jim Crace
May 2016

Chuck Newsey
The Tamale Guy

'Hasta luego.'

And the red door closed.

A little clock hung askew on the beige wall. It wasn't beige by choice, but as a result of years of tar buildup from the smoke of numerous cigarettes. They left a corrugated texture that streaked the edges of the décor unevenly. This home was one of the many small apartments cornered at the end of a long block of buildings, and was as dark and damp as the next. The little clock read 10:47pm, the little hand ticked onward, heard by Maria Vasquez.

Her husband put his duffel bag on the pavement, the contents steaming through the canvas. He locked the door and kissed the crucifix around his thick neck and placed the chain underneath his shirt. The small golden cross clung to his hairy chest that matted with sweat despite the cold Chicago winter. As he went into the night the man welcomed the chilled air. The kitchen was stifling from a full day cooking. Even when the sun went down the heat lingered, long and like a burden, in every pore, every fiber of everything when he was at home. He picked up the duffel bag and hoisted it over his shoulder. The odor was tempting, rustic, it smelled like home. Not home here in Chicago, but home in in Guatemala, a forgotten village south of Melchor de Mencos. The duffel was filled with little packets of tamales. Handmade, softened by sudor and rough palms, hand assembled by him, Jesus Vasquez, otherwise known as The Tamale Guy.

He walked to the train, locally known as the 'L', at the Western Avenue station. The Tamale Guy swung the duffel bag over the blue gate and hopped the partition. A ticket taker, smelling of smoke and with a hip of whiskey, walked over to him with slow conviction. Busted. But the Tamale Guy was ready and handed him a steaming bag of tamales. The ticket taker nodded and let him go.

The train was coming, he could feel the rumble of it approaching and quickly squealing and screeching to a halt. He ran up the stairs, two steps at a time up to the wooden platform just as the doors were sounding to close. But they weren't fast enough. Never for the Tamale Guy. He slipped through the doors and grabbed onto the metal pole as the train pulled forward towards Wicker Park. He puffed out his caramel cheeks and breathed in heavily.

'Ay Dios Mio!' he said, placing the duffel bag down and lightly slapped his round face. He huffed and huffed, inhaling deep within his body. His belly tested the strength of the zipper on his coat. He hadn't grown an inch since he underwent puberty, he stayed a husky boy as he transformed into a man. Not of body, but of mind.

This was how he met his wife, Maria Vasquez, as a boy of a man in Guatemala. She, ten years his junior, was a seventeen year old girl who had too much tequila and laid in the hay with Jesus. A cat dusted in soot hissed from behind the stack and ran out of the barn. Maria was charmed by Jesus's puerile looks, mature wisdom, and dark voice. Maria was simple, she loved Jesus. And when life got complicated with an impending life to be born from the dregs of tequila, Jesus married her. Together they decided to head north. While waiting at the Greyhound bus station in Chicago, on their way to Canada, Maria went into labor. Their journey was cut short to welcome the new life. An American life.

And his days filled with hard work. On weekday mornings, Jesus was a line chef at a diner in his neighborhood that specialized in Mexican breakfasts. He worked there until noon, when he would rush over to the sausage factory where he would stand for eight hours folding and packaging countless tubes of meat medley. In the evenings, Jesus mopped floors in the local elementary school. He would then come home to his wife who looked after a group of children from families on the block. It was a fine set-up because they were raising their own child. Jesus would deliver the children back to their homes and fall into their springy bed without an ounce of energy left. Maria would slide in next to him and wrap her body around him for the entire night. On Saturdays, Jesus would sleep until eleven in the morning, wake up, kiss his wife and child, and start making the tamales. It was the most lucrative and enjoyable job he had. He would sell them for a dollar a piece, or six for five dollars to the Chicago counterculture. It was a happy exchange for these hipster punks. They got trashed, and he would provide for them at a three hundred percent profit. It wasn't a rip off, it was quality food for small bills. Besides, making the tamales reminded him of his life back in Guatemala. No matter how much he missed it, he knew their lives were better in Chicago. *Buenos noches*, Jesus thought.

The 'L' train pulled to a halt at the corner of Chicago Avenue and North Avenue with a screech. Jesus walked out into the underground station that smelled of stale piss. The odor was worse when it was hot, and for that Jesus was thankful that it was winter. He sucked in his gut to pull his coat higher onto his neck as he walked up the stairs into the cold winter night, his duffel of tamales warm on his back.

Jesus walked around the corner and slid a little on the ice of the sidewalk. The street was dark and he couldn't see where the ice met the pavement. Down the street, the bright lights read 'Whirl-Away' in a psychedelic font with yellow neon. He kept his eyes on that beacon and shuffled his feet towards it.

Just before he pushed open the door, he paused, lifted his head high and walked into the bar. The large room was half filled with twenty-somethings, a slow Saturday for the Whirl-Away.

'Hey! Tamale Guy!' A barman grabbed a can of Pabst Blue Ribbon and handed it to Jesus.

'Gracias.'

He pulled out a few bags of tamales, moist in tiny plastic sandwich bags and held them high in the air. The aroma wafted around with the cigarette smoke, and some people came to buy his delicacy.

'Cinco dolares.' He could speak English, very well in fact. But Jesus chose not to. He thought it added to the charm of his weekend trade.

'Tamales?'

'Is it organic?' A girl with a nose piercing and jagged hair stared Jesus down. She took the bag from his hand and examined the tamales.

'No comprende.'

'Or-gan-ic, you know, like fresh and shit?' She handed it back to him.

'Lo siento, senorita.'

'Who do you think you're calling senorita?' The girl squared off with the Tamale Guy. She shrugged up her shoulders so they looked bigger, like a cat does when it feels threatened. Look bigger, ward off predators. *But cats don't have tattoos*, Jesus thought. *Cats don't know what organic means. Cats aren't dicks.*

'Lo siento, señ...'

'DON'T call me señorita.'

'Sorry.' He walked away from the girl and held up the bags of tamales, weaving in and out of small groups.

'Oh yeah, I took peyote once,' a man with a pony tail said.

'Me too. Man, that was a trip,' said another.

'Oh yeah, what did you see?'

'It's not what I saw, it's what I felt.'

'Yeah.'

'Yeah.'

'Want a beer?'

'Let's do it.'

'Bottoms up!'

Salud, Jesus thought.

They clinked their cans together. But it didn't really clink, more like a pathetic thud. It both delighted and irritated Jesus that the lighting was as dim as the conversation in these hipster bars. He headed back to the counter, and put a bag of tamales in front of the barman.

'Tamales?'

'Nah, man. I would but I'm vegetarian.'

Jesus pointed to the other barman. 'You?'

'Nah, I'm free-gan.'

The first barman offered Jesus another beer and Jesus accepted. He stuffed his tamales back into the duffel.

'Aye man, slow night. Where are the people?'

The barman pulled a ragged towel from the back of his trouser pocket, and wiped down a sticky spot on the counter.

'There's a killer show in the 'burbs tonight.'

'Burbs?'

'Yeah man, the Subject House, just outside Chicago.'

'How far?'

'I'm heading there now, actually. It's slow here, no need for two of us on tonight. No tips, so might as well get some tits!'

'Ahh, Si. Tits.'

'So whaddya say? You want a lift?'

'Muchos gracias, Señor.'

The barman threw his towel at the other man slinging drinks. 'Adios amigo!' He put a cigarette in his mouth, lit it, and walked to the door. He held it open, 'You coming or what, Tamale Guy?'

Jesus picked up his duffel and jogged to meet up with the barman. They got in his tiny car, crusty with salt from the snow plowers, and waited for the inside the heat up.

'You're a good guy, an honest man.' The barman flicked the cigarette out of the window and rolled it up.

'Thanks.'

'But if you want to get freaky on some girl tonight, I won't say anything to your missus. Cross my heart.'

'Nah, I'm vegetarian.'

The barman smiled in the dark. It looked sinister. He handed a cigarette to Jesus and lit it for him.

'You're a good guy, an honest man.'

And that is who he was— The Tamale Guy: Jesus Vasquez.

Ted Bonham
Call for Contributions

After the 'Call for Contributions' for *Magma 63*

Everybody talks, I imagine
an everywhere fog of incessant buzzing,
a radio cacophony built from the layering of many subtly
   different frequencies,
a wall somewhere between a *The Flaming Lips* live experiment
and *Lou Reed* trying to escape a record contract,
the plurality of voices blending into white noise, blank

verse used in the manufacture of what
is this? Is it a kind of art?   Well anyway,
in a buyer's market
the tone, or should we say *colour* of the voice
is a highly commercial property.
Any practicing perfectionist will tell you that

these conversations have been rehearsed within an inch of
   their lives,
starting with a question or questioning
and then falling back on Catholic guilt. Good
conversationalists are often guilty. My God
is often bored. Good conversationalists

are often good listeners,
by which I mean haven't we heard all this before?
Craving something more controversial,
we make the established noises (a loud explanation of gas)
and then sit back to wait for peer recognition.

Some of us only know what we're thinking as we're talking,
others engage in authoritative discourse
like a conversational tic—expounding on the current conflict in
   the Middle East
as a favourite party piece.
(Some themes are never out of vogue.)

All of us enjoy a good eavesdrop,
though very few have the talent to make a living out of it.
You see, ideas and conversations are inextricably linked,
albeit sometimes, it seems, by an inverse relationship,
but, whilst it is a maxim of contemporary academia to 'publish
   or perish,'
some conversations can actually get you killed.

Nicholas Doran

The Happiest World on Earth

Leo Martele stood in his board room with the Earth spread out beneath him. The sky was a dazzling, hypnotic blue while gossamer rays of sunlight bathed the pastoral lands and diamond rimmed oceans below. Legions of purple, frost-bedecked mountains let loose ribbons of sinuous rivers, surrounded by endless edens of idyllic splendour. Deserts of white sand, peppered with oases, blanketed great stretches of the southern and eastern continents, while magnificent tundras of rippled ice caked the crown and navel of the biosphere. Scattered all around the planet were glistening metropoli, each a testament of human history and endeavour. The landscapes were dotted with monolithic eco towers, providing continually optimum weather conditions across the globe. Hovering above the world were thousands of observatory stations and spaceports, while swarms of courier vessels, transport ships, security drones and pleasure cruises webbed their way across the firmament.

Leo Martele stood by his floor-to-ceiling window, looked down upon his cultivated marvel and thought: *Holy fuck, do we need more safaris!*

'Mr. Martele? Did you hear our proposition?' came a mind-vomiting sing-song voice from behind. With a sigh, Leo turned to face his delegates and self-styled 'partners' gathered around the table. Usually he had a hard time discerning one simpering yes-man from the next but he knew exactly to whom this voice belonged. He shifted his withering gaze towards the far left end of the table. Slightly obscured in the shadowed corner sat a woman so firmly bound in her pinstriped suit that he wondered if the bitch had sewn her own tight-ass shut just to fit in it. Her sickeningly flawless face was facing him expectantly, electric blue eyes boring into his.

'As I have previously stated,' he began, not wanting to meet that piercing gaze, 'Gaia Enterprises has no desire, nor need, for partnership with Clarence Voluptamatics. Now then is there any other-'

'I beg to differ Mr. Martele,' the nauseating trill continued, 'recent charts have shown an 8.785590162 percent decrease in Earth visitor attendance in the past three standard months.'

Leo closed his eyes in mingled contempt and exasperation. 'Three months ago was when the *holidays ended*!' he snarled, but the ear-raping did not stop there.

'Last year, attendance only dropped by 5.3325, the year previously by 3.44472582219001. You must face the decimals, Mr. Martele, your global tourist attraction is starting to suffer. Ten years ago, attendance dropped by less than 1 percent.'

'That was the year we opened the *Blitz Krieg Grand Europia Tour* and we're still selling H Youth outfits by the billion!'

'Um... actually, it's by the ten million now,' stammered a mousy marketing manager in the far right corner. Leo turned his icy gaze to the man, informing the speaker that he had just thrown his career down the crapper. But the damage had been done and Ms. Kimran was smiling in smug complacency.

'It's a near nine percent drop this year, Mr. Martele, just what will the drop rate be another ten years from now? Can you afford to take that risk? Can your planet?' Leo was already well into one of his routine headaches but this harpy was starting to turn it into a full-blown migraine. 'We are simply here to help, Mr. Martele. Clarence Voluptamatics proposes to increase marketing for Earth excursions by 200.803726- '

'Yes, you said as much two minutes ago!'

'Actually I originally proposed an increase of 200.800627- '

'Look, do the universe a favour and shut up that shit stirring genetic fuckup. Attendance may be suffering, but I can assure you, we are fully capable of rectifying that error without bending knees to kiss Clarence's ever more elusive ass-cheeks. Now kindly remove your own sweet-cheeks from my board room seat before you discover just how much of a fucking decimal *you're* worth!'

Ms. Kimran stood with slow deliberation but her expression did not change. She continued to face Leo, challenging his every hint of authority. 'Clarence Voluptamatics will always be open for renegotiations, Mr. Martele, and we look forward to doing business with you very soon. For the sake of your beloved enterprise, I suggest you think long and hard what form you want that business to take.'

'The only thing we need to negotiate with is whether you would prefer to exit by the door or go skydiving.'

Silence. She stood perfectly still for one whole second. Then, she moved. Not towards the door but towards Leo. What the hell was this bitch doing now? Leo made a sharp gesture to his two security composites standing by the door. The enormous labour primates grunted and made for the possible assailant. But at this Ms. Kimram broke into a fierce run, her clothes reforming in a violet flash, becoming metallic and insectoid, her face obscured in a wasp-like visage. Leo yelled but she ran right past him.

KYASSH!

The window glass shattered and the thing that Ms. Kimran had become was hurtling down towards the planet's surface. Leo watched in awestruck horror as she dived like a bullet to terra-firma. *Holy shit, she's gonna crash right into the Alexandria Resort*, he thought. But then what looked like a swarm of luminescent insects were discharged from various ports across her armour. They surrounded her, then lifted the kamikaze bitch skywards. She ascended until she was level with the naked window frame.

'*Accidents happen all the time Mr. Martele,*' the representative of

Clarence spoke in a cyber-streaked trill, *'be thankful that this last one was averted!'*

She soared upwards and was lost from view. The shattered window was already starting to self-repair itself as Leo pressed on his com-link implant. 'Security we have a terrorist breach currently hovering over North Africa. Capture her alive and incarcerate her in A-level containment, I repeat CAPTURE ALIVE!'

'It's no use,' came a drawl to his left. Leo spun around to face his health and safety advisor, who looked thoroughly disinterested by the proceedings. 'She's probably already left the atmospheric containment shield by now. There's likely to be a Clarence C. class vessel waiting to receive her just beyond our surveillance grid.'

'And whose fucking responsibility was it to keep tabs on all outer party vessels?' snarled Leo, turning his gaze towards his head of surveillance.

'S-sir,' spluttered the obese surveillance head, 'our top protocol is to ensure our outer perimeter remains free of *unsanctioned* vessels. Ms. Kimran was an invited guest and our scope does not include ships in the surrounding system.'

'Well, we're gonna have to alter that protocol now aren't we!'

'It wasn't *my* responsibility to apprehend potential terrorists,' the surveillance head retorted, pointing a stubby pink finger across the table to the chief of security, 'it was your job to keep a constant cyber guard around these offices!'

'How was I supposed to know the crazy bitch would go apeshit?!'

'Fuckups!' Leo exclaimed, 'I'm surrounded by fuckups! Ms. Kimran said that this place is heading down the singularity, and I have to agree with her on that much. Hotel Alexandria nearly suffered the same fucking fate as its bibliographic ancestor and I could have very well joined it if that bug-eyed psycho had chosen to! But more importantly, sales *have* been suffering as this oh-so-sagely-sonofabitch was courteous enough to remind us.' He gestured to the shrinking marketing manager. For several seconds there was silence. Leo turned to his minute taker, 'Strike those last four minutes from the record, Carla. Now then, what's the overall status on sales this past year?'

'Well, sir,' said an un-phased accountant, bringing up a holoscreen from her wristwatch, 'Earth pocket guides have sold approximately 1.7 trillion galaxywide.'

'Last year, it was 2.1 trillion,' Leo said.

'On the cyber-net, we've had over fifty billion downloads of Earth simulation demos.'

'That's nearly half the number we had five years ago.'

'And five years ago was a third of the numbers we were having ten years ago.'

'I don't understand,' said Leo, now pacing around the table, 'I really don't fucking understand. Over the last fifty years, I have perfected this multi-resort conurbation. Removing all impurities from the atmosphere and genetically modifying every plant to reach its maximum aesthetic potential. I resurrect classic cities, reconstruct all the world's major wonders, I even opened an Atlantis resort and spa for God's sake! I reintroduced nearly every species that had been extinct and then made up a few more. It's educational, its family friendly, you can fuck any historical figure you desire with just a simple text. Why should it be so fucking hard to market this shit?'

'A key problem arising is the influx of illegal Earth Simulations sweeping the cyber-net,' said the emaciated head of network communications.

'Illegal Earth Simulations?' said Leo, acid rising in his gullet.

'Yes,' the communications expert continued, bringing up his own, much larger, holoscreen. On it, streamed an endless tirade of advertisements. Some appeared shoddy and pixilated but most were almost perfect imitations of Gaia Enterprises' own marketing format:

New from Gaia Enterprises!!
Never step on a transport vessel ever again!!!
Holidays for the budgeters!!!
Experience the wonders of Earth from the comfort of your own home!!
We can re-render it for you wholesale!!!!

'...*What the fuck?*' said Leo, stomach acid intensifying.

'Web pirates visit Earth, collect data on particular resorts and surroundings and then construct a digital replica once they're back in their basements and mainframe vessels,' the communications expert explained. 'To begin with they were flimsy and full of glitches, only gulls bought into it. Little more than child's play really, hardly worth mentioning. Over the past several years, however, they've been getting pretty good at imitating us, in some cases seamless. Posing as legitimate Earth holiday ads was a masterstroke; approximately forty-five percent of users believe that the simulations come from Gaia enterprises.'

'But we have our own simulation demos!' exclaimed Leo.

'Yes, but these offer *complete* holidays and for a price considerably cheaper than the physical experience.'

'How the hell have they managed to pull off that level of virtual simulacrum? Our simulation demos would take years to perfect were they not designed by supercomputers. Don't these online parasites spend most of their efforts constructing their next sim-sex supermodel?'

'Ordinarily, yes,' the head of networking replied, 'but from what little we've been able to uncover on these filterers methods, it would appear that they have been receiving assistance from third party investors.'

Leo collapsed into his chair upon hearing this, massaging his throbbing temples. 'And have you been able to suss out these third parties?' he asked.

'Yes, well, some of them: Zavier interspecs, Rosedale Virtual

Living, Cryoascendancies and the Trans-Mainframe Initiative.'

Leo felt as though his insides had just done several corkscrews upon hearing those names. He was familiar with all of them; each had tried to form a partnership with him in the past. They were all far weaker than Gaia Enterprises, but Leo knew just how savvy these techsploitation companies could be when negotiating a business partnership, so he had declined all their offers. Now they appeared to have all joined forces by distributing these virtual imitations, but why? Surely there were other corporations to take advantage of. How much of their resources were they spending in creating these simulations? And all through the guises of online hacks. It just didn't sound practical. And how could they, rival companies, have all partnered up just for this? What was their overlying directive? Then it hit him, like a titanium glove to the face.

'*Clarence,*' he uttered in cold fury, 'all of them have become subsidiaries of Clarence Voluptamatics!' A tide of murmurings erupted across the boardroom. Sounds of shock, some of fear and a few, Leo detected with rising apprehension, of excitement. '*So,*' Leo boomed over the chatter, 'Clarence is trying to run us into the ground. What initiatives have we got to combat this?'

'Nothing new as of yet,' said the head of communications, 'each time we try shut down one of these simulations, they divide into several new programs, each with a different form of encoding. In addition, many of them have viral defence mechanisms. If someone tries to tamper with them, these viruses get released into the invading system and spread like Feranian Plague. Remember that mass blackout and weapons malfunction across Chinaland a few months back?'

'Ok, so fighting them directly is useless, any other suggestions?'

'Has anyone considered, distributing complete virtual holidays ourselves?' piped in the fired-to-be marketing manager, desperately grasping at any thread he could reach.

'And defeat the purpose of visiting us at all? Why don't we

just nuke the whole fucking planet while we're at it? Save us all the trouble of hiring a demolitions team!' shouted Leo in exasperation.

'I suppose the only other option,' said the still un-phased accounted, 'would be to take Clarence's offer and form a partnership.'

At this the room buzzed with murmurs of agreement, even enthusiasm. Leo seized the nearest '*I HEART EARTH*' mug and hurled it across the table. Everyone ducked and leaned out of the path of the souvenir projectile. It smashed into the deluxe omni-pigment screen where it remained lodged.

'We're just gonna play right into the hands of that corporation devouring bastard?! We're just gonna abandon all we've built in these past decades? We hand the keys over to Clarence and he'll turn this place into the next Planet Tengoku!'

'The fact in all of this is, sir,' drawled the health and safety advisor. 'that a partnership wouldn't affect any of us in the least. If anything, our salaries will be increased. The only person who stands to lose anything in all of this, *is you*.'

Leo gaped in horror as heads began nodding all around. 'You make one move towards Clarence,' he said, his voice shaking somewhat, 'and I'll fire the whole damn lot of you!'

'Fire us and your beloved enterprise really will collapse,' the advisor chuckled, 'and you won't find another person in the whole galaxy who won't simply be bought by Clarence when the time comes.'

His zeal not completely evaporated, Leo raised a quavering hand towards his health and safety advisor. 'You've just been waiting for this to happen for years, haven't you?'

'Quite, frankly, I think we all have,' the advisor smirked, looking around the table. More nodding heads. More murmurs of agreement. 'In fact, now that I think on it, you're the only person standing between us and sealing the deal.' A collective murmur of consent. People were starting to stand now.

Leo got to his feet also, lost for words as his delegates turned on him one by one. But then he sighed, moved towards the window and took one last look at all he had built. One last look at his beloved Earth. He could hear the clacking of firearms being drawn from behind. He knew when he was beaten. In the end, he was just one more digit on the decimal...

Helena Hoar

The Cradley Tragedy

It was called The Cradley Tragedy by the newspapers. In the summer of 1906 The Advertiser and The Stourbridge News and the County Express chewed on mouthfuls of it for three weeks, panting after the story as it revealed itself through stabbings and shootings, murder and suicide. It finished with the funeral of twenty-six year old Caroline Pearson.

Poor Caroline, dead and undiscovered in a field for a fortnight, her body so rotted away it was not possible to tell how she had been killed. The accounts of the day say she was a good looking woman, that she took care with her appearance, but in the single photograph the papers reproduced it is difficult to see her attractions. And her body was so badly decomposed when it was found that it would have been too hard to lay her out, wash her and dress her in her best.

St Michael's, where she is buried, is on the top of Brierley Hill. It's easy to pass by it without noticing. The church and its large churchyard isn't visible from the main road, shored up by a high embankment, spread across the brow of the hill. The war memorial, a uniformed soldier, faces the road; Caroline was dead before the war, the chainmakers' strike, women's suffrage. The site is hugged tight by houses, roads, shops, but the churchyard is beautiful and calm.

There is no politeness about this place, no gravel paths or ancient yews or tended gravesides. The beauty does not lie in the brutal church either with wire across its stained glass and the strange blocks of additions that confuse its identity; from the north side it does not look like a church at all. Its beauty is its position, high up and looking to Cannock Chase in the north, and to the south, behind the Brierley Hill flats and the STD Carpet Warehouse, there are the Clent hills and Clee and the Malverns. Gala Bingo and the market hall obscure Merry Hill. In Caroline's time the view was a conflict of field and furnace and mine. Among the flats is Little Potter Street, a scrap of a street name from Caroline's day where her friend Alice lived in the poor housing where many of the brickworkers lived with their dishevelled morality. From far away the rain is coming in.

There is beauty in the graveyard too. The unmown grass clumps in tussocks. Badgers have dug divots up to feast on the fattened worms. Butter yellow beech leaves fall in the breeze and mast is dense on the chest tombs. An ash tree twice as tall as a person has thrust through a stone lid and a row of headstones is deep within a bramble bush. Here, on Thursday 12th July 1906 Caroline was buried, among the people of the parish with their sturdy Black Country names, Bache and Cartwright, Pardoe and Pargeter, Holden and Elwell and Flavell. The headstones tell where they lived, George Fereday of Moore Street, Annie Bloomer of John Street, grounded and never moving so that the street they lived in was so integral it became part of their name. It is less than a mile from here to where Caroline lived. Caroline Pearson of Turners Lane. And gently, gently the bones, the stones are all rusting back into the earth.

The Reverend Herbert Henville Dibben led her funeral service. 'It is the saddest thing I have ever had to do,' he said, and went on to rage against drinking and immorality, his church overlooking the slums then as it overlooks the flats with its single parents and drug users now. Black Country workers, Caroline too, believed they'd earned a drink after a day toiling, and each week the papers listed police court reports of drunkenness and violence from men and women.

People are using the churchyard as a cut-through to the fading high street. Parking is free on the short road outside the church.

Along here, and in the church, and in the cemetery over a thousand people crowded together to witness Caroline's funeral. The papers reported that they wanted to show their sympathy towards her. The papers reported that they wanted to show their sympathy towards her, but, after the weeks of excitement, it is hard to imagine sympathy was the only reason that the mines and chain shops and brickyards were quiet the day.

Olivia Hodgson
The Mechanic

After Heaney

You were the one for revamps. I would watch
As you polished the wooden wheel, sipped Scotch,
Through window-light, like glowing citrus rind,
Clasping keys, or cleaned up iron oxide.
I learned no more observing this master
Shamble through, caress the oil disaster,
Than he grazing through my guide, 'Poetics':
'Well, I measure far better in metrics.'

Yet our metre to have and miles to hold
Still-birthed: forced to Warwickshire's fringe.
This found prejudice, mechanic control:
A clamp on which your closing judgements hinge,
And those kisses flecked with petrol
On the back seat of broken things.

Olivia Hodgson

Digbeth

When the gaping church door let
a sparing sigh,
I found Digbeth animate,
 curling from the bricked arch girdle.
Aorta'd city: I found you
in a state of peace
for once, for once.
Ringing with the sincerity
of a silversmith's blow,
the sound washed the stars
from the air
and placed them
for a new engagement ring.
The smoke blew from a cigarette
as the factory's chimney split the sky.
One enveloped cut: invitation to the city.
A sip on the choke of the air;
a finger to the lips of traffic.

Rhoda Greaves
Sunday Roast

Remember that time Dad made you eat your dinner outside? He called you a farm animal. Usually it began with 'effing' when he was *that* mad. It must have been a Sunday as you had on a do-up shirt and I was wearing my red velvet dress. We'd just got back from Sunday school. Remember those colourings we'd done? Of the loaves and fishes? You were only allowed crayons at home, but the vicar's wife – was she really called Mary? – She'd let you use pens and you hadn't made a mess. Mum put them on the fridge with Pac-man magnets, and when we showed Dad he just laughed out loud. Asked us, didn't we know God was dead? Asked Mum, why was she filling our heads with that shit.

You told him you were a Christian: had tasted the blood and the body. Because he was laughing, you didn't know not to. And that's what started him, you eating Jesus. I could see it in his nostrils and the way his left eye twitched. He wouldn't say anything though, not until we were all at the table. Not until he could turn it into something else, like chewing your food without sealing your lips.

Richard Hughes

The Passion of Dr Abacus

FADE IN:

INT. DR. ABACUS'S BASEMENT - DAY

Black. And we are falling out of a newspaper clipping that reads: 'YOU CAN ALWAYS COUNT ON DR. ABACUS!'

Below is a picture of the beefcake, in glasses and lab-coat, lifting a laughing President Barack Obama over his head.

The rest of the room is overloaded with Dr. Abacus memorabilia -- trading cards, comics, toys, and a life-size cardboard cut out.

Dr. Abacus looks serious on the cover of Time Magazine's Person of the Year 2015...

And sultry as the winner of People Magazine's Sexiest Man of the Year 2015. 'HIS STEAMIEST INTERVIEW YET!'

DR. ABACUS is looking on his past glory from a wheelchair. Raw eyed. Haggard.

DOORBELL.

>   DR. ABACUS
> Leave me alone.

DOORBELL. DOORBELL.

>   DR. ABACUS (CONT'D)
> Fuck off!

A BLAST upstairs causes dust to dance down.

Manipulating the joystick of his electric
wheelchair, Dr. Abacus slowly turns around to face
the basement door.

Colossal footsteps draw near.

>   DR. ABACUS (CONT'D)
>   Oh no...

BOOM! The basement door is blown off its hinges in
a nebula of wood and dust.

It clears slightly. A film of dust coats Dr.
Abacus.

>   DR. ABACUS (CONT'D)
>   Hello Iggy.

A giant mass is silhouetted where the basement
door once was. It's not human -- but it is roughly
shaped like one.

It speaks low and slow. Voice RUMBLING like an
earthquake.

>   IGGY
>   You don't answer phone! You don't
>   answer door!

>   DR. ABACUS
>   I know. I know.

>   IGGY
>   No. I don't think you do.

The dust clears fully. The light shifts. We see
IGGY THE IGNEOUS ROCK FORMATION.

She tries to shimmy through the door. CRASH.
Drywall crumbling. Dr. Abacus winces.

She's on the stairs.

>   IGGY (CONT'D)
>   You're being an...

She smashes her head on the low ceiling. MOANS.

IGGY (CONT'D)
Asshole!

The stairs collapse and she disappears.

GRRRROOOOAAANNN.

She bashes her way out. Losing her balance, she staggers around the room smashing up the place.

DR. ABACUS
Why are you here Iggy?

Iggy rights herself.

IGGY
Major Overkill. She's back.

DR. ABACUS
What is this, some kind of joke? I have a TV, Iggy.

Dr. Abacus's wide screen TV, cracked and spitting electricity following Iggy's rampage, falls from its wall mount to the floor.

DR. ABACUS (CONT'D)
I know she's back.

IGGY
Well, what you gonna do about it?

DR. ABACUS
Oh, I don't know. Maybe I'll schedule a showdown for two p.m.? In fact better make that three. Nurse Sarah comes round at two to CLEAN THE SHIT OUT OF MY PANTS!

Dr. Abacus redirects his chair to avoid Iggy's gaze.

IGGY
But... I know you can beat her. I've seen you stop bullets with your... your... Taliban penis.

DR. ABACUS
Telekinesis.

He sighs.

DR. ABACUS (CONT'D)
It was my faith in telekinesis
that put me in this chair.

BEGIN FLASHBACK

EXT. DOWNTOWN NEW YORK CITY - DAY

Buildings and cars burn. The streets are churned to rubble.

Dr. Abacus stands with hands on his waist. His lab-coat billows in the wind.

DR. ABACUS
Your bullets are useless Major
Overkill.

The villainess MAJOR OVERKILL levels her sawed-off-shotgun at Dr. Abacus. She is a walking armoury. Her tank top reveals humongous biceps.

DR. ABACUS (CONT'D)
Do your worst!

The barrel of the shotgun EXPLODES, blowing Dr. Abacus away. END FLASHBACK

INT. DR. ABACUS'S BASEMENT - DAY

IGGY
Yeah, that was pretty
embarrassing.

Dr Abacus's chair WHIRS as he turns back to face Iggy. A fresh tear-track runs down his dusty cheek.

DR. ABACUS
It's over, Iggy.

                    IGGY
          Don't say that. You're a doctor.
          You can fix yourself.

                    DR. ABACUS
          I'm a doctor of dental surgery.

                    IGGY
          Oh.

Iggy is desperate.

                    IGGY (CONT'D)
          I've always thought you had nice
          teeth.

                    DR. ABACUS
          I don't operate on myself!

He starts WAILING like a child. Iggy slumps her shoulders. A beat. Then -

Iggy draws herself up to her full height, eyes glittering.

                    IGGY
          Have I ever told you about how I
          got like this?

Dr. Abacus quietens. SNIFFS. Shakes his head.

                    IGGY (CONT'D)
          Three hundred years ago I had it
          all.

BEGIN FLASHBACK

EXT. BASE OF VOLCANO - DAY

A tiny wooden shack sits at the base of a massive volcano. A plain woman wearing peasant clothes milks a goat. This is Iggy. Her HUSBAND smokes a corn cob pipe.

                    IGGY (V.O.) (CONT'D)
          A husband. A goat. A shack at the
          base of a beautiful volcano.

INT. DR. ABACUS'S BASEMENT - DAY (PRESENT)

               DR. ABACUS
    What happened?

               IGGY
    The volcano erupted.

EXT. BASE OF VOLCANO - DAY

BOOM! The volcano erupts. Lava spews. The sky turns black. A huge rock falls from the sky, crushing her shack.

Lava flows down the volcano engulfing her husband, her goat and finally Iggy herself.

INT. DR. ABACUS'S BASEMENT - DAY (PRESENT)

               IGGY (CONT'D)
    I should have been dead. But I was
    alive. Somewhere. Inside the rock.
    But I couldn't move.

Intrigued, Dr. Abacus leans in. EXT. BASE OF VOLCANO - DAY

               IGGY (V.O.) (CONT'D)
    I had to learn everything again. A
    hundred years went by...

A time lapse shows a century passing. The lava flows cool. The rock hardens. Days, months and years whizz by. The landscape subtly changes.

               IGGY (V.O) (CONT'D)
    I got so angry at times. So bored.
    But I learnt to take things slow.
    Boredom turned to peace. Anger
    became a smaller part of me.

The earth begins to shake. Deep fissures form in the rock.

               IGGY (V.O.) (CONT'D)
    And finally... I rose.

Fissures form a crude stencil outline, like a gingerbread man imprinted on dough. Iggy MOANS as she wrenches herself free from the earth.

She stands. CRACKING as she flexes her limbs. Her face is bathed in golden sunlight. Her eyes open for the first time.

END FLASHBACK

INT. DR. ABACUS'S BASEMENT - DAY

                IGGY (CONT'D)
    So you see. I don't believe it's
    over.

Iggy turns away from Dr. Abacus. She rummages through the rubble she's created.

                DR. ABACUS
    Iggy, you're a good friend. But
    I'm not... Wait. Iggy. What are
    you doing? NO!

Iggy hurls a huge piece of debris at Dr. Abacus. He raises his arms to shield himself.

The debris doesn't reach him... It hangs in the air, turning as though floating in space. A beat.

WOOOOOOOO! Dr. Abacus and Iggy holler like frat boys who have just finished off a beer bong.

The floating debris is dashed against the basement wall.

                DR. ABACUS (CONT'D)
    Okay, let's do this!

Looking around at his ransacked basement.

                DR. ABACUS (CONT'D)
    But where? We can't train here.

Iggy has a knowing expression.

                IGGY
    I know the perfect place.

EXT. BASE OF VOLCANO - DAY

Iggy's new and improved shack, complete with a barn, sits at the base of the volcano. A winter wonderland -- snowcapped trees, icicles hang from roofs.

MONTAGE - TRAINING (ROCKY 4 PARODY)

INT. BARN - DR. Abacus holds a skipping rope looking unimpressed. Iggy's new goat BLEATS at him.

INT. BARN - Dr. Abacus dangles upside down from a hayloft as Iggy holds his feet.

EXT. SHACK - Dr. Abacus tries to chop wood. The block gets stuck on the axe.

INT. BARN - Dr. Abacus attempts to lift a mound of rocks via a rope pull. Gets dragged out of his chair.

INT. BARN - Dr. Abacus turns this way and that with a yoke on his shoulders.

INT. SHACK - Dr. Abacus balls up an old picture of himself stuck to a mirror. Sees himself reflected.

INT. BARN - Dr. Abacus skips by levitating.

INT. BARN - Dr. Abacus, his feet held by Iggy from a hayloft, levitates his body to complete a sit up.

EXT. SHACK - Dr. Abacus levitates the axe. Brings it down on a block of wood, splitting it asunder.

INT. BARN - Dr. Abacus levitates the mound of rocks.

INT. BARN - The yoke gets thrown to the floor.

WOODS - Iggy runs through the wood. Dr. Abacus is on her back, head poking out of a huge ruck sack. They stop at a bog. Dr. Abacus levitates an X-WING from its depths. High five.

ICY ROAD - A black car follows Dr. Abacus. They both speed up. Dr. Abacus takes off. The car crashes into a snowdrift.

PANORAMA - Dr. Abacus flying over beautiful countryside.

VOLCANO TOP - Dr. Abacus bellows victoriously.

END OF MONTAGE.

EXT. DOWNTOWN NEW YORK CITY - DAY

A legion of armed soldiers in jack boots stand to attention. They are focused on a stage in front of them.

A GENERAL in a decorated black uniform addresses the company from a podium.

> GENERAL
> This is our time...

FOOTSTEPS. A pair of boots make their way to the stage.

> GENERAL (CONT'D)
> The age of strength...

Tenement buildings rise either side of the company. They are draped with the image of Major Overkill flexing her muscles.

> GENERAL (CONT'D)
> The age of force...

Children peek through curtains. Mothers pull them away.

> GENERAL (CONT'D)
> The age of power.

The boots climb the stage steps.

> GENERAL (CONT'D)
> Brothers. Sisters. I give you the orchestrator of our time... Major Overkill.

The company performs a salute in perfect unison. The General steps down from the podium.

The boots CLUNK across the stage. It is Major Overkill, wielding a mini-gun. She takes to the podium.

>   MAJOR OVERKILL
> Thank you General. But let me make one thing clear.

A look of anxiety passes over the General.

>   MAJOR OVERKILL (CONT'D)
> This is not our time.

The barrel of the mini-gun WHINES as it begins to turn.

>   MAJOR OVERKILL (CONT'D)
> This is my time!

She turns and fires. The gunfire illuminates her face -- one of relish. The General is reduced to a puddle of gore.

Some of the less experienced soldiers look nervous.

>   MAJOR OVERKILL (CONT'D)
> Is that understood? This is my time!

>   DR. ABACUS (O.S.)
> Your time will soon be over, Major Overkill.

Dr. Abacus and Iggy approach the rear of the company.

>   IGGY
> Because you'll be dead.

>   DR. ABACUS
> That was implied.

Recognising the duo, Major Overkill gives a wry smile.

> MAJOR OVERKILL
> Ah! Dr. Abacus. So you've come to die.

> DR. ABACUS
> I've come to teach you a lesson.

> IGGY
> Like you can't go around paralysing people and expect to get away with it.

Dr. Abacus looks at Iggy in disbelief.

> DR. ABACUS
> It doesn't sound as cool when you over-explain everything.

Major Overkill rolls her eyes.

> IGGY
> I just wanted to make sure she...

> MAJOR OVERKILL
> KILL THEM!

The soldiers cock their weapons. A beat. RARRGGH! Iggy charges. Dr. Abacus WHIRS forward.

GUNFIRE. Iggy breaks through the company like a juggernaut. Bodies fly. Bullets chip away at her rocky frame.

Dr. Abacus produces a force field. Bullets dissolve before they can reach him.

He begins to glow an eerie blue. Brighter and brighter. Major Overkill shields her eyes.

He fires a blinding pulse that knocks out all in his path.

The pulse reaches Major Overkill. The stage EXPLODES. Major Overkill is hurled through the air.

She hits the ground. HARD. She isn't moving. A beat.

She peels herself off the pavement. Broken and bloody. Behind her, Iggy is chasing off the remaining soldiers.

The mini-gun begins to WHINE as the barrel turns. It falters. Broken. But there is another WHINE -- Dr. Abacus's electric wheelchair approaching.

> DR. ABACUS
> It's over.

> MAJOR OVERKILL
> It's not over till I say it's over.

> DR. ABACUS
> I admire your resolve.

Major Overkill drops the mini-gun. She draws a sawed-off-shotgun from her leg holster. Admires it.

Dr. Abacus looks nervous.

> MAJOR OVERKILL
> Remember this?

Iggy sees what's happening.

> DR. ABACUS
> You should not forget the past.

Major Overkill takes aim. Iggy is running to help.

> DR. ABACUS (CONT'D)
> You should learn from it.

The barrel EXPLODES. Everything is in slow motion. The shot begins to slow down... it stops... and begin to reverse!

Major Overkill's face turns from relish to horror. The shot eats away at her face.

Back to full speed and her head explodes. She collapses.

Iggy appears at Dr. Abacus's side. A beat. They give each other a sober nod.

They walk and wheel into the low, evening sun.

FADE OUT.

Joe Legge
Bethany

Bethany claimed an empty table in the hall, opened her princess lunchbox and peeled cling film off of her sandwiches. Hovis Best of Both with a bright layer of strawberry jam oozing from the bread and landing on one of the folding tables at which other children were sitting and eating their lunches. She liked her lunch box. It was a Disney one she had made her parents buy for her before Year Four started two months ago. The princess on the cover was Rapunzel from Tangled, Bethany's second favourite film after Brave. She had green eyes, was very beautiful, and had long blonde hair. Bethany believed the resemblance between the picture on the box and the box's owner was obvious.

'Can we see it?' Her friend Nicole whispered over the din of other girls and boys finding their friends and swapping packets of crisps for chocolate bars.

'Not yet.' Bethany watched the sour faced lunchtime monitor walking in the direction of their group. She unzipped her backpack below the folding table, her hand gripping the canvas top and holding it upright.

Kirsty arrived, removed her indicatively large lunch box from her own bag, lowered herself into a chair and squeaked it closer to the table.

'Do you have it?' Now Bethany was whispering as Kirsty set a used Fanta bottle on the table. Glue residue from the torn off label had been blackened by fabric fibres and the contents had been replaced over and over by whatever Kirsty's mum told her to fill it with before getting her out of the house. Her mum was too tired to get the Ribena bottle out of the cupboard over the sink this morning so today she had water.

'Yeah.' Kirsty said, 'Is that enough?'

Bethany considered the bottle, three quarters full.

'Yeah.'

The lunchtime monitor turned away from the trio and marched in the direction of some boys throwing food at each other. Bethany looked at her companions and nodded. She silently slid her chair back and held her bag between her legs. She opened it to reveal a small white box made out of the shiny thin card her mum's mobile phone came in. Lumps of dry soil had spilled out and muddied her spelling book. A dusty odour of pencil shavings and used erasers had mixed with whatever was in the box and floated up as Nicole and Kirsty leaned in. With the steady hand of a bomb disposal agent she had seen in a film her dad was watching one Saturday, Bethany opened the lid.

'Is it there?' Nicole said, peering in close enough that her brunette split ends almost mingled with strands of shredded newspaper, the only contents that was visible.

'Yeah,' Bethany shot a glare at Nicole before turning to address Kirsty. 'Move the paper. It's probably gone to sleep.'

Kirsty shifted forward.

'Slowly!' Bethany hissed.

Three curious prods of Kirsty's chubby fingers revealed a clump of light brown fuzz the size of a golf ball with a tiny beak on one side and two pea sized eyes as shiny and lifeless as marbles.

'Is it sleeping?' Nicole's stare was fixed on the baby bird but she had started to back away. The sound of other girls playing outside floated in with the warm summer air and Nicole looked towards the door.

'Yeah.' Said Bethany, not taking her eyes from the bundle of fluff and paper. A bitter stench from the box was growing thick in the girl's nostrils. 'I'll just-' and she nudged the box as gently as though she were negotiating a particularly risky Jenga block.

Nothing happened. She jiggled the box, paused, and then shook it harder. Her smile vanished.

'It's dead.' Nicole announced, and looked again towards the playground door.

'No it isn't.' Bethany said and bounced the box until strands of newspaper fell onto the tops of her legs.

'Shall we give it some water?' Kirsty offered, hoping to rescue Bethany and be the hero of the afternoon.

'It's dead.' Nicole confirmed and tears began to form in Bethany's eyes.

'It's your fault, Kirsty.' Bethany said and shut the lid. 'You put your bag on mine in assembly so you killed it.'

'No I didn't.' Kirsty said, 'I was sat near the front so I put my bag there!'

'Then,' Bethany said as she shoved the box back in her bag, 'it was when you poked it. You tried to wake it up but you killed it.'

'I didn't!' Kirsty's words came out louder than she had intended.

'You did, Kirsty.' Nicole joined in. 'I saw you.'

'We both saw you.' Bethany said. She knew from Blue Peter that she shouldn't have taken the baby bird, but it might have died on the ground, and if she saved it then it could be her pet like Pascal in Tangled. But now it was dead, and Bethany didn't know the punishment for bird killing. Killing people means you go to prison and sometimes hurting animals means you go to prison. It would be better if Kirsty went to prison instead of Bethany because Kirsty is fat and not as clever so it wouldn't matter as much. But who decides if you go to prison? She thought it was either the Prime Minister or the Queen. It must be the Prime Minister for boys and the Queen for girls. And Nicole was already on her side so Bethany could get Nicole to tell the Queen it was Kirsty's fault. Two against one.

Bethany stopped crying and dusted the last few fragments of soil and crumpled newspaper from her lap and smoothed the wrinkles out of her skirt. Kirsty continued trying to get Nicole to believe it wasn't her but Nicole kept saying 'Yes it was. *Yes*, it *was!*'

'Right.' Said Bethany over the others. She was back in control and turned to Kirsty. 'You've got to bury it so nobody ever finds it.'

Kirsty's lip quivered and Bethany finally picked up her sandwich.

'Why has it got to be me?' Kirsty looked from Bethany, to Nicole, to her hands.

Bethany bit into her food. 'Because otherwise we'll tell everyone you're a killer.'

Jack Warren
All my mates have become clowns

Laura has perfected a custard pie recipe that is both
delicious and low fat. I take one to the face every two
hours and the carpet is filthy. As I cannot drink
I am often the designated driver of the clown car. Kofi
performs pratfalls all evening and lets me win at pool,
he is starting to suffer from back pain and the make-up
is ruining his complexion. When I cannot leave my room
Kai & Kate bring me balloon animals. They have been late
for work twice this week although their poodles are
beginning to show signs of real emotional acuity.
Everyday there is more glitter in the kettle and everyone
is exhausted. I am starting to resent the need for clowns.

Jack Warren

Self-portrait as Digbeth Branch canal

Silent gunmetal waters, I have seen my face in you.
I have smelt the timber yard taint of creosote
on winter nights as yellow feathered herons
stood stoic among the meadowsweet and black bricks.
This is where the city keeps its derelicts.
Jaundiced men burning polythene sheets in the underpass
razor wire nodding in the wind as soot stained
factories hold the ache of rain.
Out here there is a glimpse of the unheralded,
of offal and bleach, coal and steel.
I am beginning to make myself at home.

Jack Warren

Preparing for spring

The rain blackens roots. Deifies the grim.
One lone hubcap in the mud. A crow carcass
slackening in the soil. In the distance
a tower block bullies the skyline, a windowless
garage squats in the street level decay of cellophane
and plastic bottles. I have lived in cities too long,
have reneged on secret promises to myself
made in earnest under the dog star,
have forgotten the feel of sphagnum bog on
bare feet and the anonymous tranquility of
a hidden trail away from all this.
In two months I will sleep under a cherry
tree as it foams into life.

Dan Witherall

Release

FADE IN:

INT. UBER. DAY.

The taxi rolls to a stop in front of JEREMY (23, broken, defenseless, raw).

He wears a suit, unprepared for the pouring rain. He doesn't even notice the car. He stares around him as if seeing it all afresh.

> DRIVER (O.S)
> Alright mate? Where to?

Jeremy pauses. He doesn't know.

> DRIVER (CONT'D) (O.S)
> You wanna just get in, yeah?

Jeremy doesn't, but nods shyly as he gets in anyway.

Across the road, TOM (22, tracksuit, pruned) stares over at him, checks his watch.

EXT. PARK. DAY.

AMAAN (22, boyish, athletic, fearful) jogs between trees, wipes the downpour from his brow.

He aims for puddles, mud stains his legs. He stops, leans over, gasps for breath.

The muddy puddle below him offers a distorted reflection.

EXT. FRONT GARDEN. DAY.

Amaan approaches his home, takes his keys out. And stops. Tom stands at his door.

>AMAAN

Hi.

>TOM

Amaan! Mate! Where you been?

Tom hugs Amaan. Amaan doesn't hug back.

>AMAAN

Uh, just around I guess. Nowhere.

>TOM

I know, man. No one has seen you.

>AMAAN

Yeah. I guess...

>TOM

Well, people stop calling, after a while.

>AMAAN

Yeah. It's my fault.

>TOM

Nah. It isn't.

>AMAAN

So, how you been?

>TOM

Never mind me. How're you?

>AMAAN

I'm alright.

>TOM

It is so good to see you! You're looking good. Lost a bit of weight, but...

>AMAAN

Yeah.

Amaan is folding in on himself. Tom sees it.

> TOM
> Uh, so... do you know?

> AMAAN
> Know what?

Tom considers his approach. His facade fades. Eventually...

> TOM
> Well... he's out.

Amaan's eyes glaze. Terror calmly floats in.

> AMAAN
> What?

Tom consoles. Amaan backs away.

> TOM
> I saw him.

> AMAAN
> When?

> TOM
> Earlier. I don't have your number anymore so I thought I'd --

Amaan gasps for breath. Tom moves in closer.

> TOM (CONT'D)
> Listen. If you want me to -- I mean, we'll all take care of him if you want.

> AMAAN
> No.

> TOM
> I mean, he won't come near you anyway. He won't dare. But if you want --

> AMAAN
> No. Please.

                    TOM

     No?

                    AMAAN

     Uh...

Amaan collects himself, avoids Tom's eyes.

                    TOM

     Well?

                    AMAAN

     I forgive him.

                    TOM

     What?

                    AMAAN

     I forgive him.

Tom stares at Amaan, appalled. Baffled. Amaan stares to the ground, ashamed. He heaves --

                    TOM

     Am --

-- And vomits.

EXT. HOUSE. DAY.

Jeremy watches from across the road. A detached, well-kept home leans over him. He's weary, yet drawn to it.

THEN --

Jeremy stands at the open door with a MAN (60's) who holds garden sheers.

                    MAN
          Oh, no, we bought this place about
          three years ago.

Jeremy nods. He's pieced it together. He smiles sadly as he steps away.

                    MAN (CONT'D)

>   You know, it was only about two
>   months after we moved in that we
>   found out. Someone down the local
>   told my wife.

Jeremy turns to leave.

>   MAN (CONT'D)
>   Said they left because they
>   couldn't stand the shame of what
>   their son had done.

Jeremy exhales loudly, nods as he walks away.

>   MAN (CONT'D)
>   That's you, isn't it?

Jeremy reaches the pavement, quickens his pace.

>   MAN (CONT'D)
>   Please, don't ever come back here!

INT. KITCHEN. NIGHT.

TARUB (late 40's, mourning, guarded) prepares dinner. She stands passively, like a doll.

Amaan appears, lingers by the door. Tarub springs into upbeat mode when she sees him.

>   TARUB
>   Hello darling! Did you have a good
>   run?

Amaan can't hide it. Tarub knows. He breaks down into tears. She takes his hand, comforts him. She's used to it.

>   TARUB (CONT'D)
>   Oh sweetheart! It's okay, it's
>   okay.

INT. LIVING ROOM. NIGHT.

Tarub and Amaan sit formally on the sofa. Amaan avoids his mother's look of concern. Tarub sips tea.

Eventually...

                    AMAAN
          He's out.

Tarub flinches. She slowly rests her cup on the floor. Without looking, she takes Amaan's hand again.

INT. BEDROOM. NIGHT.

Amaan sits on his bed, cuddling a pillow. His eyes stare widely at thewall ahead. A noise. Outside. It breaks Amaan's trance.

Amaan stands at the window, staring out. He stifles his gasp.

Jeremy stands outside, staring up. His gaze on Amaan is a fixed point in time.

Amaan clasps his eyes shuts, inhales deeply. It's happening. Relief. Release.

He's ready.

He opens his eyes. But --

Jeremy is gone.

Amaan leans against the window, searches down the street. Nothing.

He turns toward the bed. It is suddenly UNMADE. Blankets twisted, the indents of two bodies made out in the loose sheets.

Amaan steps away from it.

His stare paralysed on the sheets, he slides down the wall.

EXT. PARK. NIGHT.

Jeremy slumps drunk on a bench, throws a cigarette to the floor and watches the embers die.

He swigs from a bottle of rum. It dribbles

down his chin. He wipes it off, lights another
cigarette.

LATER --

Amongst the woods in the b.g., Jeremy settles
under a tree. He lays his suit jacket on the floor,
and lies on top of it in the fetal position; his
back to the open grassland.

In the f.g., the bench is littered with a cluster
of cigarette butts, and the empty rum bottle.

EXT. PARK. DAY.

Jeremy sits back on the bench. He's a state.

He checks his watch, rubs his face, collecting
courage. He slowly nods to himself, and stands to
leave.

INT. LIVING ROOM. DAY.

Amaan, exhausted, carries two plates from the
kitchen to the dining table.

He sets one plate down and glances outside.

He stops dead. The plate in his hand crashes to
the floor.

> TARUB (O.S.)
>
> Amaan?

Tarub comes from the kitchen to investigate, sees
Amaan staring.

She comes closer, follows his eyes to the window.
Outside, facing them from the street: Jeremy.

Tarub instantly makes for the door.

> TARUB
>
> No!

The door opening snaps Amaan out of it. He chases
his mother.

                    AMAAN
               No, mum, no!

EXT. FRONT GARDEN. DAY.

Tarub bursts out of the front door, charges at
Jeremy.

                    TARUB
          Stay the fuck away from my son!

Jeremy doesn't flinch.

Amaan runs out after Tarub. His eyes meet Jeremy's
and he startles back momentarily.

                    AMAAN
               Mum, please!

Tarub belts Jeremy across the face. Jeremy is
struck backwards. Tarub doesn't stop.

Amaan tries to hold Tarub back. She swings at him
-- red mist -- and hits Jeremy hard again, who
falls to his knees.

Amaan can only watch. He's in total shock. Tarub
spits on Jeremy, lunges at him.

                    TARUB
          You ruined my boy's life!

Tarub can't stop. Neighbours peak from their
windows. Jeremy says nothing. Just stares at
Amaan.

                    TARUB (CONT'D)
          I swear I'll kill you!

Amaan clutches his mouth, wailing tears. He stares
back at Jeremy.

                    AMAAN
               Stop!

Amaan jumps between Tarub and Jeremy. Tarub's
momentum can't be stopped, and she slaps Amaan
HARD, across the face.

She stops, shocked.

> TARUB
> Get out of my way, Amaan.

> AMAAN
> No. I can't.

Tarub is enraged, distraught.

> TARUB
> This man destroyed us, Amaan.

She flings Amaan aside, he lands on his knees, hopeless.

> AMAAN
> He's done nothing wrong!

A beat. Silence. Tarub freezes.

Jeremy's gaze drops to the floor. Finally.

Tarub kneels with Amaan, touching his chest, unable to process.

> TARUB
> What are you even saying?

Amaan stares through Tarub as he breaks down.

> TARUB (CONT'D)
> My sweet boy, talk to me. Please.

Amaan draws breath to speak. But he doesn't need to. A beat. Tarub can't comprehend it. And then she can.

> TARUB (CONT'D)
> You...?

Amaan nods.

> TARUB (CONT'D)
> Why didn't you...?

Amaan sinks. It's out there.

                    AMAAN
          I was ashamed.

Tarub looks over to Jeremy. He is bloodied,
broken. Tarub almost goes to him, but turns back
to Amaan as she stands.

                    AMAAN (CONT'D)
          I was ashamed, mum.

Tarub takes a moment, thinks on her words. Her
eyes flush with tears.

                    TARUB (CONT'D)
          Well. I wouldn't have been. Not of
          that.

She takes a step back. She needs to escape. She
marches back inside, slamming the door behind her.

Amaan is in total dismay. Jeremy rises to his
feet. Amaan doesn't look up.

                    AMAAN
          I'm so sorry.

Jeremy just stares ahead.

                    AMAAN (CONT'D)
          I'm so sorry.

Finally, Jeremy glances his way.

                    AMAAN (CONT'D)
          Why did you take the blame?

The hint of a smile flashes across Jeremy's face.

MONTAGE OF FLASHBACKS:

A) - A younger Amaan, Jeremy, Tom and others drink
in a pub. Amaan tells a story, catching Jeremy's
looks as he does.

B) - Amaan and Jeremy share a joint. Jeremy
strokes the back of Amaan's hair as a smile
lingers between them. Amaan breaks the moment.

C) - Amaan enters a pub to see a woman hanging on Jeremy's arm. Jeremy catches his jealousy.

D) - Amaan smokes a cigarette outside, watching Jeremy say goodbye to the woman. He smiles as Jeremy turns to approach him.

E) - Amaan and Jeremy lie in bed, lost in their moment.

G) - Jeremy kisses Amaan goodbye. Amaan turns, sees the two outlines in his sheets seen in Scene 6, and regret overcomes him.

END FLASHBACKS.

Amaan sits on his heels, staring desperately up at Jeremy.

              AMAAN (CONT'D)
  Why?

Jeremy stares back blankly. He opens his mouth, clears his throat.

Eventually...

              JEREMY
  I loved you.

Jeremy exhales loudly. He looks around him, unsure which way to go. Finally, he starts to walk away as Amaan looks on.

              AMAAN
  I was scared. I was so scared!

Jeremy doesn't look back.

              AMAAN (CONT'D)
  Please come back! Please come
  back.

Jeremy wipes the blood from his face. Behind him, Amaan weeps, his head on the ground.

Jeremy reaches the end of the road. He looks to each side, choosing his path.

                    AMAAN (CONT'D)
          Don't leave me.

But Jeremy is gone. And Amaan knows he always will
be. Neighbours now tentatively surround Amaan. He
doesn't notice

-- just stares ahead at the empty street corner.

FADE OUT: THE END.

Jan Barker

At the Edge of my Mind

It's always the same. Do you think you can help me?

Beneath the harsh afternoon sun, the red plastic football bumps and rolls down through the sea-grasses and between the folds of the dunes towards the beach.

I hear other families on the sands, laughter and voices competing for attention, the whacking of ball games. Music clashes between radio stations against a backing track of screeching gulls. Waves surf in to scrunch and drag on pebbles at the shoreline. I play alone in the grainy sand mixed with grit and shells and sea-glass, digging with a red plastic spade and small fingertips. Secretly I build a protective moat around myself. In the humid high of summer, every movement is wading through soup.

At the edge of my mind, I'm waiting for that moment when it's time to leave the beach; when mummy will push on my red jelly shoes. Not soft like the jelly after school. Hard and plastic and lumpy where the sand seeps inside. First she'll rub my feet with the towel that I hate, thin and white with orange palm trees. It feels rough and mean. She'll rub my toes which are crooked like my dad's and I'll wriggle and squeal, the towel brisk and sore on my skin. But it won't make any difference.

'Please don't rub my feet, mummy, it hurts.' If I struggle too much there will be a small smack on my leg. I'll be funny about people touching my feet for the rest of my life. She'll bend my arms into my tulip-red cardigan. I like red but it's too hot to wear today. I'll try to explain. But it won't make any difference. So I try not to think about that moment when it will be time to leave.

Before that moment, on the beach, mummy is singing along to Dusty on the radio. I know that song is one of her favourites but it sounds sad to me. She reaches for my hands to pull me from the secret moat. I know the words and sing and I try to dance but I can't in the sand and I fall over and pull mummy down too but she laughs and so I'm not in trouble this time. The music on the radio is warm treacle in my ears. I'll dance to that song for the rest of my life.

At the edge of my mind, I'm waiting for that moment when daddy wants me to go into the sea. He'll run into the waves and I'll follow, reluctant. I don't like the sharp stones, they make my feet sore. Daddy will swim around and splash me and laugh at me and try to teach me to swim. I'll try, but it will frighten me and I'll panic.

'I don't like the water; don't hold me down, daddy.' Daddy will get impatient and head in to shore and I'll trail behind, pushing through the shallows on to the sand. I'll be afraid of the sea for the rest of my life.

Daddy is running about playing with the red plastic football. It won't be long until he wants to swim again. He likes doing backstroke. So to keep him on the beach I join in running along and catching the red ball and throwing it back and I like that daddy seems pleased and we play together like that for a while. Mummy is singing along to 'Shout' with Lulu and I join in the chorus and mummy and daddy build sandcastles with me. With yellow and orange buckets, we carefully construct the turrets on the biggest sandcastle in the world. Daddy says the moats I build around the castle are really good. This is the best thing about being on the beach. I'll love making sandcastles for the rest of my life.

Mummy and daddy were always telling me not to worry. I heard the doctor tell them I was an over-anxious child, but I didn't know what that meant. I tried to please them because pleasing adults seemed to be what was expected. I didn't want to spoil the day on the beach.

Mummy says she's going to fetch ice creams and do I want to go with her. I want to stay with Daddy because I'm too hot and I feel a bit funny. My eyes blink and everything looks too bright, like I'm watching us on the telly. Mummy fumbles for coins in her brown purse with the zip that sticks. She scrambles in the sand to stand up. I watch my mother walk away in her crinkly red swimsuit, the one which ties behind her neck. I hear daddy behind me, singing along to a song that I don't know. He's adding a new wing to the sandcastle and asks me to help him finish it.

It's in that instant, or maybe in the next, that I become aware of the change.

I can still see mummy, in her crinkly red swimsuit with the halter neck, buying strawberry ice-creams at the beach kiosk. She turns and waves while she's waiting for our three-penny

cornets. Why doesn't she come? I try to call her but I don't know how to speak.

I feel clammy and spiky and frightened. That's the moment. When I disconnect.

Daddy is looking at me with a puzzled expression. Something is wrong. I can see his lips talking at me, the question in his face. Then he's shouting. Daddies aren't meant to be frightened. I wish I could hear him because then maybe everything will be all right.

But it won't make any difference.

The sky has turned from its usual yellow colour to something less than black. Daddy is reaching out but I'm inside a silent storm of nothingness. The sea, burning orange, pours into the moat around the biggest sandcastle in the world. I hear it sucking and swirling and sliding away.

Then daddy has disappeared. Or maybe he's behind me. But if I turn around and daddy's not there and mummy hasn't come, then my last moment of hope will be snatched away. So I never turn around.

And the moments I'm dreading at the edge of my mind – moments with the jelly shoes and the mean towel and the sore toes and daddy in the sea - those moments never come again.

My world tilts and skews and I'm cold beyond cold and a tiny movement in my peripheral vision pulls my eyes to the right. And beneath the harsh afternoon sun, I watch as the red plastic football bumps and rolls down through the sea-grasses and the folds of the dunes towards me.

It's always the same. They say I've gone bad but I don't know what's real anymore. I don't remember hurting anyone.

Do you think you can help me?

Joel Rawlin

The Girl from Work

She'd only started last month. The assistant; the boss's 'right-hand man' but really a faceless machine like the rest of us.

She sits beside me at company meetings and we mutter obscenities through clenched jaws, 'Have you seen how Tom's been looking at the intern? That perv. He's three times her age.', 'How can Deborah say we've all been putting the work in? She only turns up once a week, lazy cow.' We stop after the glares became relentless.

At lunch we laugh and joke. We talk about ourselves, ask questions and relax. We share stories about our lives, our memories and occasionally we share a glance into each other's eyes and it holds.

Then, like every other weekday, we say our goodbyes and part ways.

She goes home to her empty flat, I go home to my wife.

We sit in silence and eat. I wash up as she pours a bath. I put on the football until she comes down and we turn it to one of her programmes. I used to enjoy the compromises. The meals at fancy restaurants; even though I suggested a curry in front of the T.V. The films at the cinema which I had no interest in seeing. The family visits when I could be out with friends.

Then we make love; whisper that we love each other but I think of the girl from work. I could love her. Not yet, but one day maybe.

Jim Crace
1, from *The Devil's Larder*

Someone has taken off – and lost – the label on the can. There are two glassy lines of glue with just a trace of stripped paper where the label was attached. The can's batch number – *RG2JD* 19547 – is embossed on one of the ends. Top or bottom end? No one can tell what's up or down. The metal isn't very old.

They do not like to throw it out. It might be salmon – not cheap. Or tuna steaks. Or rings of syruped pineapple. Too good to waste. Guava halves. Lychees. Leek soup. Skinned, Italian plum tomatoes. Of course, they ought to open up the can and have a look, and eat the contents there and then. Or plan a meal around it. It must be something that they like, or used to like. It's in their larder. It had a label once. They chose it in the shop.

They shake the can up against their ears. They sniff at it. They compare it with the other cans inside the larder to find a match in size and shape. But still they cannot tell if it is beans or fruit or fish. They are like children with unopened birthday gifts. Will they be disappointed when they open up the can? Will it be what they want? Sometimes their humour is macabre: the contents are beyond description – baby flesh, sliced fingers, dog waste, worms, the venom of a hundred mambas – and that is why there is no label.

One night, when there are guests and all the wine has gone, they put the can into the candlelight amongst the debris of their meal and play the guessing game. An aphrodisiac, perhaps: 'Let's try.' A plague – should they open up and spoon it out? A tune, canned music, something never heard before that would rise from the open can, evaporate, and not be heard again. The elixir of youth. The human soup of DNA. A devil or a god?

It's tempting just to stab it with a knife. Wound it. See how it bleeds. What is the colour of the blood? What is its taste?

We all should have a can like this. Let it rust. Let the rims turn rough and brown. Lift it up and shake it if you want. Shake its sweetness or its bitterness. Agitate the juicy heaviness within. The gravy heaviness. The choice is wounding it with knives, or never touching it again.

Jim Crace
2, from *The Devil's Larder*

'*This is for* the angel,' Grandma used to say, tearing off a strip of dough for me to take into the yard. 'Leave it somewhere he can see.' Sometimes I left the strip on the street wall. Sometimes I draped it on the washing line. Sometimes I put it on the outside windowsill and hid behind the kitchen curtain beads to spot the angel in the yard.

Grandma said I wouldn't catch him eating the dough. 'That's only greedy birds,' she explained. 'The angel comes to kiss it, that's all, otherwise my bread won't rise.' And, sure enough, I often saw the birds come down to peck at our strip of dough. And, sure enough, my grandma's bread would nearly always rise. When it didn't she would say the birds had eaten the strip of dough before the angel had a chance to prove it with his kisses.

But I never saw an angel on the windowsill. Not even once.

The thought of the angels in the yard terrified my girls and so, when we made bread – in that same house, but thirty years along the line and Grandma long since gone to kiss the angels herself - I used to say, 'To make good bread I need an angel in the kitchen. Who'll be the angel today and kiss the dough?' My girls would race to kiss the dough. I'll not forget the smudge of flour on their lips. Or how, when I had taken the scarred and toppling loaves of bread out of the oven, they'd demand a strip of hot crust to dip into the honey pot and wipe around the corners of the pâté jar. This was their angel pay. This was their reward for kissing.

Now there are no angels in the kitchen. I'm the grandma and the girls are living far too far away to visit me more than once or twice a year. I'm too stiff and out of sorts to visit them myself unless I'm taken in a car, but I don't like to ask. I stay in touch in a car, but I don't like to ask. I stay in touch with everyone by phone. I keep as busy as I can. I clean, although the house is far too large for me. I walk, when it is warm and dry, down to the port and to the shops and take a taxi back. I keep plants in the yard in pots and on the windowsills. I eat mostly out of a can or frozen meals or packet soups.

This afternoon, I thought I'd fill my time by making bread. My old wrists ache with tugging at the dough of what, I think, will have to be my final loaves. I tore a strip off for good luck, kissed it, put it on the window-sill. I warmed the over, greased the tins, and put the dough to cook on the highest shelf. Now I'm waiting at the window, with a smudge of flour on my lips and with the smell of baking bread rising through the house, for the yard to fill and darken with the shadows and the wings.

Gregory Leadbetter

Imp

On the bad days, I shooed her mews away
out of nothing but an absence of joy.
I never installed a back-door flap for her,
so she would patter all night to get in at the window
while I lay wide-eyed and sleepless, pretending not to hear.

I know it was a blessing
when she landed like a fly on my forehead
as I was trying to write,
her cicada rustle scribbling in and out
before the flick of my hand sent her to hide
in the plumbing, where she whined for weeks
until I found her, toad-shy and morning-blind
in the kitchen sink. I held her, for the first time then,
revived her with what has become her favourite wine.

It has often been her game
to go missing. It is where she thrives,
as if she delights in being imagined –
looked-for in the fading light,
or at the beck of a buzzard's call.
In the garden, I would find her spraint,
stinking of rotten fruit and putrid grain,
the tang of iron and the fume of honeycomb.
She would announce her return with a black-out
bite through electrical cable, then creep in close, dab
my eye with a spider-leg to see if I was awake.

She could drive me mad
with her cuckoo blink –
then I remember how she would
pull me out of the O of a dream
when I couldn't breathe
and make me a day-bed from her sloughed skin.
She would lap at whatever saltwater
leaked from me. It wasn't right
for her to see me cry,
but she would tongue my tears away,
curl me a rabbit-fur snake
for a pillow and blow through my ears.
Her opalescent gaze could break
the world-egg open
over and over again.

Tonight, I will leave out a bowl
of blood and marrow to tempt her back,
fall asleep on the sofa, wait
for a child's hand to touch my face.

Gregory Leadbetter
Stalking

Between the fingers of the falling dew
I find a path that takes me through
the sleeping eye to where it wakes
on the other side of the dream it makes

I tread the moss that beds the hoof
I follow into absent proof
a moth without a moon
a wanderer with the day's wound

my fingers are lichen and as slow
my mirror the yew that blisters shadow

the gift I bring for the darkling birth
is stillness suckled from my breath

I spring the roe and the world in hiding

Siren Knight

Noir

It is always night time here but you'll be surprised how quickly your eyes will adjust to the darkness. And when they have adjusted and your dormant senses have converged, you are going to have to make a decision.

You might choose the broken pathway that leads up into the mountains. Or you may take your chances in the misty forest, acquiescing to its bad habit of reaching forward and beckoning in. There is always danger at a crossroads, yet there is no redemption to be claimed on either roadway here.

So I implore you to wander, with no path to guide you. To plunge into the no-man's land that resides on each side of the road. To submit to the dread in your stomach and let it act as a compass that navigates you through the night.

Heed warning. There is an ochre stench that lingers on the air, so billowing and thick that it must be pushed aside as you walk. But keep your mouth and your mind closed here, you do not want to give audience to the things that wait in its pockets.

There is a danger that needs no introduction. It is a demanding thing, a jealous thing and it already claims your attention. You know of what I speak. That place where your eyes are drawn. Where there are black fires that burn on the horizon. When it ends you will have no choice but to go to them, to the creatures that reside there, for how else will you barter your escape? They will watch you. From within the hollows that linger in shadows of where their faces once were. Hollows that drip with blood when they are full from the feed. If they claim you, you are to be one of them. And no struggle will allow your body the luxury of an escape. Your mind will be offered in sacrifice to them.

If they do not, you are prey. And the last thing you will hear is the way your bones squeak and snap like firewood and a pain you could not describe even if they *had* left you your tongue. And a stench so sick you will welcome the smell of your own sweet blood being spilled.

If you were smart, you would never have come. You would never have clambered up out of your nightmare, with your gnarled little fingers and into the darkness to be here.

But you are here… you silly little thing. Here is where you are.

So you turn back. You flee to the embrace of what you once knew.

But the crevice that you crawled through is now nothing but a dark chasm in a dark wall that offers no promise of release. You are trapped. You press your palms to a solid wall. There is no give, there is no hope of return.

So maybe you resign yourself to your new plight and glance around you for places to take shelter, things to eat. Is it possible to stay here? Can you make a life here in this darkness? Can you pull it up around your ears and brave sleep? Would you dare eat the scurrying varmint that roam here? Or risk to drink from the dark waters that run off jagged rocks into pools of black?

You could try.

Try to make a home in the darkness. You could hope that the hooded creatures don't make it this far out. But how long will your heart beat in such a sorry state? How long before you crave the touch of another, before food and water are no longer able to sustain you? Before you forget how to bend your arms into an embrace? Before your skin forgets how to identify warmth?

So surely you must continue moving into the no-man's land? Ignoring the salacious whispers of the misty forest that croon sweet nothings into your neck. Ignoring the seduction of the broken steps of the mountain that whisper of the unknown. For to venture either way will surely mean death...or worse.

Yes, you must push further, with nothing but the thick yellowing stench of the open land to keep you company. Push your way through it, retch when you need to, and wade on. You might notice that the horizon gets closer, not like in that other world where you never seem to be able to reach it. No, here you will advance upon the great black fires burning clearly in the darkness and the hooded things that tend them.

Those creatures on the horizon.

There is no sneaking up on them.

They see you way before you see them...they see you now.

They taste your blood on the air, it calls out to them.

Careful now, not too quickly. Don't you see? If you move like prey, then that is what you are.

The fear is beginning to overcome you now isn't it? Creeping up and down your body, deep inside your clothes, slithering against the cold sweat of your skin. Dread snakes through your stomach lining, skulking in between each wretched organ.

The shadows lick against your body as you walk, pay them no heed. Keep your mouth closed, keep your mind closed. Do not listen to the charming voices of the night. Keep focused, do not stray left or right, follow the dread, follow the dread, wade through the stench, listen to the things your goose bumps whisper, listen to the way your stomach clutches at your ribs. Those are the details that will show you how to fear, they know of what you approach.

When the moment and your footsteps finally collide and you gain the horizon, you will stand before the gathering of the hooded creatures and you will have to make your choice. You must select and advance upon one, even if your legs quiver beneath you, even if your ankles threaten to give way. Choose the creature that stoops in an almost familiar way, as if it is a shadow of something you once knew. And you must look into the monster. Do not get distracted by the ever burning black fires to the left and right. The glowing darkness will try to steal your focus, will try to blind what you know. Instead, you must stare into the hooded face, stare into the gaping holes, and look past the blood that gushes out of them.

Do not stare at it, for then they will surely corrupt your mind. You must look past it, look into the core of it. And with all your might you must whisper aloud its secret. The secret you knew the minute that you arrived here. The secret that was prowling along your mouth the whole time. That they were once just like you. Those creatures. Just like you. A thing of flesh and blood just like you. Stumbling across a darkness in a recurring nightmare. That they once had eyes that did not pour blood, and mouths that spoke words instead of warbled calls. That they once could taste food, grip pride, feel the touch of another with senses that would not turn to ash as they held someone close.

You might watch the orifices widen and reach out for words that they can no longer give voice to. Watch as the hooded figure is angered at the memories you provoke, at the way you poke and expose its vulnerabilities. Watch as it plunges forward to feed on your flesh, to cage you forever. You must stand firm and only then, at the very last moment, when all hope is gone, when they are inches from you and you stare certain death in the face without flinching. Then! Then is when you must throw away all hopes of life and returning home...you must plunge this scroll, this map of secrets, into the very depths of the shadows of its face. Feel the crack of the parchment crashing through the hollowed eye socket. Let it pierce through it, as you turn on your heels and you must run, run, run back through the no-man's land, through the thick stench, run, no straying to left or right, no retreating into the whispers of the mountains or the beckoning of the forest. You must run. Run back until you see the dark wall, see the shaft of light twisting through the crevice, and know that the portal opens for you. Clamber through it, make your body fit the chasm, contort yourself to fit and tumble back into the recurring nightmare you climbed out of, the one you've had since childhood, you know the one. Cling to it! Embrace it as your own. Don't let those terrible fingers pull you back. Watch them crumble to ash as you pass through the fracture. And wake up, wake up little thing. You must wake up out of your nightmare, the one you know.

Shirley Lloyd

Pause

'I'm not looking for a relationship.' Kimberley's gentle but determined words, slid off her tongue and were immediately consumed by Matt's kiss. He stopped briefly to acknowledge her statement with a slow and breathy,

'Okay.'

Weekends with Matt were always adventurous. From deliberately hiking off designated trails to camping in the most off the beaten track locations. There were spontaneous trips to different cities to watch a foreign film, and jaunts to the coast on days when temperatures reached below zero. Her secret nickname for him was Mr. Everywhere.

Their conversations never lacked stimulus, as most subjects they discussed was imbued with his vast knowledge. However, despite this it felt like he filled every pause with words. There was the odd occasion when Kimberley thought, if only he'd stop talking, for just little while and allow some space for silence. But she never said anything. Instead she decided that it was a free country and who was she to stop him.

Kimberley's time spent with Matt was a complete departure from her previous dating experiences. Although she was close to her parents and siblings, they were unaware that she was seeing someone. When asked what she was up to, she gave a this-and-that type answer, and knowing how private she was they didn't pry.

Matt was an alternate weekend Dad and had been for over four years. The first time they met for a coffee he talked openly about his two kids, and showed her pictures of them, on his mobile phone. He clearly led an organised life, placing the needs of his kids as a top priority. The descriptions of his weekends with them were also action packed. He would drive two hundred miles north up the motorway, pick them up and drive them back to their second home. Mondays were extra early starts for the return journey to ensure that he got them to school on time. Matt often shared how the kids were progressing at school, and in their individual extra-curricula activities, but the idea of Kimberley meeting them was never broached, either by him or her.

Then, eight months on since their first coffee, on one of those wintery Sunday evenings, just after dusk. That time of the day when the Sunday blues creeps in and intrudes upon the remnants of a weekend. Everything between Matt and Kimberley, from their most intimate moments to mundane domestic tasks had a comfortable flow about it. Kimberley was now packed and ready to leave for home. They performed their Sunday farewell ritual and kissed passionately, and as their lips reluctantly separated she looked into his eyes, but instead of their farewell ending there she whispered,

'I really love being with you.'

As the last word escaped from her lips she watched the signature glint in his eyes ebb away and Matt paused.

Tony Howe

Arle

Hectares of cultural inertia pricked
out in pushchairs and crushed men
in charity shop combos: that black

raincoat pink cap patent shoe look.
The Matrix is always down for
essential maintenance here – no pop-up spaces;

only the off-cuts passed over
by Wimpey Homes. Territorial offal.
Bureaucrats, thankfully, will never extol us
asvibrant.

Jack Roberts
Spectrum

Felix Abernathy could feel sweat running down his side. The air con was broken and the engineers had been in everyday for the past week trying to fix it. Up and down ladders behind him, scrambling for tools and disappearing into the mysterious spaces above the ceiling panels. His cubicle was in the centre of the office. No windows to open for a gentle breeze, and all the fans had been scurried away by management into the boardroom. The admins were in today, reluctantly mingling with the drones who did their dirty work to ensure they broke their necks getting the Spectrum Annual Report in before the deadline.

Then there was Felix; his eyes feeling swollen and painful from the harsh lights. Typing away then highlighting what he had written, copying and pasting it into three separate tables that were then directly messaged to the next cubicle for citation and editing. It was a monotonous task. A conveyor belt of sullen faces filled the room. The only sound allowed was the low hum of calls being taken. Even the phones were connected to headsets so the constant ringing from the guys downstairs wouldn't disturb them.

The one unique feature of Felix's cubicle, was the direct line of sight of the target screen that hung above the glass panes of the boardroom. It flipped between the number of calls taken and dropped, and the level of progress being made on the report that day. Wedged in the centre of four clocks, two left and two right, that told the time of four different countries. He didn't care what time it was in China or Germany, he doubted anyone did. That is, apart from the suits that had begun to congregate around the screen. Pointing at the screen and then conferring with one another, occasionally making subtle glances toward particular drones. Fortunately, not in his direction.

It was them. The Big Five. The Spectrum. Clones dressed in the same black suits with tactically sharp haircuts and a tablet each. The only difference between them, aside from their physical appearance, was the colour of their ties. Felix, like many of the drones, had been forced to learn from the handbook who each admin was. There was no point in remembering their names. They wouldn't bother to remember his. But the ties said it all. They couldn't be just colours. Everything had to be jargonised. The ties distinguished rank. The colour allocated a position in the upper echelons of the corporate ladder

Fuchsia was the lowest, but the first guard at the gate. Then came Cyan, a number cruncher. Emerald, the only woman on the team, had her hair cut into a severe bob that rested on her shoulders. Office legends spread about her clawing her way to the top. The amount of backstabbing and manipulation was tremendous, but worth every penny for her now six figure salary. Wine, the red tie, was far older, with wispy, silver hair and a drooping eye lid. He was just a book keeper and minute taker during the early years of the company because of his excellent memory. Obviously a tactical positioning, Felix thought. He wasn't just a doddering old man with a good memory. He needed appeasing so the secrets wouldn't come bursting from the floodgate.

The final man cast an imposing presence. Obsidian, the stony faced black tie. A buzz started around the desks about a year ago that he was given the nickname 'undertaker' by a drone. Due, in part, to the fact he looked as if he was going to a funeral. It couldn't have been a coincidence that said colleague who came up with it was ushered out, with just enough noise to prove a point for the rest of them to stay in their place. Felix' tie (for anyone who cared) was the same as every other drone. Provided upon employment in a vacuum sealed bag, and labelled as

'Bastion'. A shade of filthy grey not too dissimilar to clay.

'Felix. Psst Felix.' A whisper came from the adjoining cubicle.

'What is it?' Felix whispered back, ducking his head around to ensure there were no lingering ears.

'Don't you think it's strange that the Spectrum want this report so quickly?'

'Tom, it's a report. I don't ask questions, I just pass the buck to the next poor bastard.'

'Which happens to be me! So you should care.'

Tom O'Donovan, always looking for a way to worm out of the machine. There was no such thing as doing less work. You shirked, you were out. His desk said it all. While Felix had everything filed and organised under sticky notes, and in draws and filing cabinets, Tom had paper littered everywhere, coffee rings on half of them and his complimentary pad of sticky notes had become a pornographic flip-book. After seeing those stick people going at it so many times, the novelty had worn off.

'Shh, get back to it. Undertaker's doing a sweep.' Without even checking if this were true, Felix forced his eyes back to the screen: copy, paste, enter, delete. Copy, paste, enter, delete. Repeat, repeat, repeat. Obsidian was indeed doing a sweep of the cubicle maze. Peering round the corners of the door like a spectre, with Emerald and Fuchsia close behind him, shoulder surfing. He peered round into Felix' space. He could feel the pressure of their presence but tried his best to ignore it, tapping his same pattern of keys.

'You.' His voice was low and dry, as if he had been gargling sand. 'Abernathy isn't it?' Felix whirled round on his chair and stood to attention, fixing his tie and making a vain attempt to ruffle his scruffy hair into neatness.

'Yes sir. Felix.' He stuck out a hand to shake. An impulse. Maybe he shouldn't have done that. A second had passed. The longest second. Emerald twitched an eyebrow. Instant regret.

'Felix. You don't hear that name every day.' He finally reciprocated the hand shake with crushing force. No smile. Strictly business. 'Felix, the report is nearly complete. We need the first fifty percent of it physically taken to the archive. Can you handle that?'

'Absolutely sir.' With no hesitation, Fuchsia dumped a cardboard box on the edge of the desk.

'Your colleague, Mr O'Donovan-' Tom had peeked his head over like a muskrat at the sound of his name. '-will be transcribing for the remainder of the report in the Digitisation Department.'

He gave a sharp turn to Tom, who nodded and sunk back down behind his protective wall, all the bravado leaving him.

'Both of you ensure that you are done within the hour.' He skulked off, his lackeys behind him.

Felix lifted the box from the desk, almost crumpling to the floor with its weight. He and Tom didn't say another word as they passed Wine and Cyan. The corridor out of the office was as clinical as the inside. Whitewash walls with grey ceiling tiles and the same disgustingly bright lights.

'See you on the other side buddy.' Tom gave a grin and waved himself into the lift and the end of the left intersection. Felix returned the pleasantries and went to the right. The archive was not as impressive as it sounded. A plain, square room that Felix had been in before with filing cabinets and cardboard boxes reaching the ceiling. An old computer was pushed back into the corner with a flickering green curser against a black screen. In this archive, the annals of the company's history resided.

Felix dumped the box on the floor and removed its contents. A stack of papers with the company's official logo on the front. A line of five colours. Fuchsia, Cyan, Emerald, Wine and Obsidian and the word Spectrum written underneath it. Great. Felix thought. More junk that'll be stored away never to be seen again.

He replaced the lid and lifted it onto the lowest pile, the easiest for him to reach. Not so easy. He caught the edge of the box underneath. The weight pulled it down, littering the floor with paper.

'Shit.' He muttered. He began scrambling the papers together, but they all looked the same. No telling which order they had been in.

'Shit, shit, shit.' The quick organising had started. The flicks of the terminal curser were catching him in his peripheral vision. So much so that he could count them. A flick a second. Sixty flicks per minute. He had counted eighteen-hundred clicks by the time he had got down to the last folder on the floor. Still plenty of time to get back to his desk and chew the fat with Tom.

He clung to the last folder which appeared different to all the rest. It was bound with Spectrum tape. Unopened and dustier, a faded red 'classified' mark on the front. It was one he'd seen before, but not for a long time. Perhaps a detailed manifesto of his superiors cooking the books. Or a dossier of where the bodies are buried, if at all, there were any. Felix stared at it for longer than he should have but with little hesitation, put it back in the box. Five years at the company and he was past caring. Curiosity was something he had lost long ago. Whatever was in there was beyond his concern, and he liked to keep it that way. He turned off the light and locked the door behind him.

Richard Hughes

Summer Vegetables

Fruit flies, like airborne comma splices,
plague the leukemic leeks and leprosied parsnips.
They are on them and before them
like an ironic, malevolent mosquito net.
They are in them. Or rather they are
in the shallow sheen that once was
all leek, all parsnip,
now a crude cordial of dissolution.

We quarantine the best we can
but we are a business and vegetables need
to be sold, sold quicker for their condition
worsens! We flay the leeks and castrate
the parsnips' slippery and quivering genitalia.
Then, once again, they are publicly presented
in all their silent mutilation.
(I feel a human emotion
for the swedes and carrots
left untouched at either flank.)
Only the aesthetically terminal are removed
and their gangrene is hacked off with a margin
of good flesh: bagged chunks sold for cheap
like hunks of miscellaneous dog meat.
Only when the see-through-plastic bags become stomachs
of putrefaction are the remnants of the summer
vegetables committed to the outback bin,
to sit atop broken crates stacked like unlit pyres,

atop the mass graves of a strawberry holocaust,
gestating in their dead, translucent wombs,
unwetted by the summer rain.

Nicholas Doran

Enker Green

Grendel gazed into the emerald abyss. A green that eclipsed all other greens. His mind lurched as he tried to comprehend that brilliant shade- no- *principle* of green. The colour had come first, exploding out of his consciousness, even before the ground had collapsed. *Collapsed...* was that the right word? No, it was as if the colour had forced its way out of the ground. And not just the ground but through the seams, the very molecules that wedded the tapestry of reality together. Much less a pit than a tear in the universe. All that Grendel could grasp about this other world was... *green.*

A car alarm went off a few streets down. Grendel remembered where he was and spun around, seeing if anyone had come to investigate the eldritch blaze emanating just feet away, but there was nothing. He stood alone in the forsaken park. Not even a band of intoxicated skin-heads had chosen to haunt this particular barren stretch. Not tonight anyway. That was why Grendel had picked this place to begin with: it was so unremarkable, so infinitesimal in the great urban sprawl enclosing it, that the common pedestrian barely acknowledged its presence. Especially after dark. Perfect for a bit of late night experimentation. Now though, he was certain that within seconds people would be flocking towards him and his newfound green hole, whipping their phones and cameras out. Within a minute it would go viral and then... it would be over for him.

And yet still no one approached. Grendel scanned the area in all directions.

Then understanding came: if he, a person of brilliant mind

who could conjure and bind arcane power to his will, who had witnessed and experienced wonders and horrors that would cause most men's sanities to liquefy, if such a person as *himself* could perceive nothing other than a colour from this unhallowed realm, what would a passing street walker see? A spurt of green at the back of their minds? And then back to the London night life, nothing to see in this council-neglected park apart from some ginger-haired youth in a black leather coat, staring at a dark patch on the ground.

Grendel couldn't relax though. This wasn't what he had intended. All that was supposed to happen was for the rune leaf to call up an entity *from* the Green Realm. But instead he was stuck with this gaping rift. Well, he thought, he'd best make the most of a reality-tearing situation. That leaf had cost him too much to obtain to just flee the scene and do nothing. He looked down at his palm where the rune leaf was still laid bare. Its surface was a vibrant, practically glowing, shade of green. A pale reflection of the *true* colour oozing from the ground. The Gaulish symbols had vanished, and the leaf's veins now pulsed crimson. Grendel had paid gateway's tithe in blood and he expected profitable results. He was going to forge a connection with this realm. Of that, he was determined. He was going to gain access to its immense power.

He took one cautious step towards the green hole and with that the depth of the colour intensified. He resisted the pull of green oblivion and then spoke in a slightly high but resolute voice. 'I invoke the power of the *Enker-Grene*.' Emerald spikes drove into his brain, into his soul. *But no*; he had to resist. He had come so far. He was so close now. 'I seek an audience with the equinox court.' He hoped this rough English translation would suffice; his woefully crude Celtiberian was probably the reason for the rift opening up to begin with.

The colour pulsed and fluctuated through his mind in rhythmic time. Grendel staggered and tried to comprehend the meaning behind it. Rather than fight against the green, he closed his eyes and disconnected from his sensory stimuli, a trick any mage worth his fire-salts could accomplish with ease, and focussed on the oscillating colour. Then he heard the laughter. It wasn't so much he heard but rather that he felt the laughter ringing through his mind as one with the colour. The realm was belittling him, but he did not flinch. He was only mortal after all- *for now at least*. This could only be expected from such a power. From such a collection of powers.

How many times had they dealt with his kind? Thousands? Millions? Probably very few in recent centuries, but then what were centuries to *them*, to *it*? And for that matter, how many other worlds had made similar contact with the Green Realm? Hundreds? Billions? And where did this plane of existence rank amidst the great astral ocean of realities? Probably grouped within a pocket cesspool of other mediocre worlds. Any thoughts of indignation for this mocking display were likely to have his soul reduced to celestial compost. He let the laughter reverberate through his psyche.

Green seeped in and spread throughout his very being. And the green knew him. There was nothing for Grendel to hide. No point in trying to deceive. Jade venom swam through his brain and Grendel almost screamed. But he stood firm. He must prove himself worthy of the *Enker* if he was to have any hope of making rapport. Any hope of survival. The venom collated in his neurons, invading his mind with new ideas. No, wait. *Speech*. The realm was now speaking to him.

'*The equinox court has addressed you, Grendel Juventino Hopper, and has deemed you worthy of its sport,*' the Green sang and/or transmitted. '*The council shall now send forth a herald for your amusement. Does this please you?*' Grendel desperately thought of every concept of reverence he could conceive. '*A simple yes or no would suffice,*' the Green Realm jeered.

'*Yes*,' Grendel uttered.

'*Then enjoy*,' sang the choir of infinite green. And with that, the colour retreated from his mind.

But the green hole remained. Grendel waited, his eye sockets slowly roasting from the extended exposure to that terrible colour. Then the reality tear began to move. To convulse. It was as if the portal was undergoing contractions. Trying to birth something into this world. Grendel prudently took one step back but then found that he was unable to lift his other foot. The colour was not finished with him yet.

The green receded; normality seemed to return to the park. Then the green erupted. An aspect of the realm broke free from its gestalt and forced its way into the world. Grendel would have cried out if he could relate such a response to this aberration, to this thing which flouted the very definition of *being*. Tendrils of green energy lashed out at Grendel, binding him and lifting him upwards. How high up he did not know. Ten feet? A hundred feet? Beyond the earth's orbit? Time and space had quickly become inconsequential concepts to this aspect of emerald infinity. The thing towered above him, stretching endlessly in every direction, its form constantly shifting. But always were there eyes. Or at least what Grendel could only assume were eyes. Millions of them. Scrutinizing his mind, his desires, his passions.

He struggled to maintain his rationality but what did such trivialities matter when faced against this Envoy of the *Enker Grene*. '*Too much*?' whispered a thought at the back of his head. Grendel's mind began to lapse into oblivion. '*Very well*,' the envoy said/ transmitted in a dejected tone.

The green vanished. The tendrils relinquished their embrace and Grendel fell back. The stars returned to the night sky. The sounds of London traffic resumed their discordant symphony and cool inflexible ground made contact with Grendel's back.

Grendel groaned, both in blessed relief and from a fatefully placed broken bottle sticking into his back. Fortunately, it had not torn through his leather coat. He sat up stiffly, trying to regain his bearings and then crawled back in shock, shrieking in pain as the splintered glass made contact with his buttocks. For where the green rift had once been, there was now an immense tree standing in its place.

But it wasn't just a tree, it was a person too. Each of the branches was an arm. The trunk was a perfectly toned body, flawless in both masculine and feminine respects. The many leaves that adorned its head were each a separate being in their own right but also were they part of the whole. Spiritual aspects of the envoy. Each dancing to their own tempo, independent of any breeze.

But it was the face that caused Grendel to retreat. Comprised of tangled twigs and collated foliage, twisted into a monstrous countenance that vaguely mimicked *or mocked* a human visage, it looked down upon Grendel and smiled. Its mouth stretched and expanded in a grin that would snap a human jaw. But these were mere artifices compared to its eyes, burning with that terrible colour. Each cornea a portal to the Green Realm.

The tree-thing's roots caressed and swam through the earth. They slithered around Grendel, playfully prodding and stroking him. The sensation was far from pleasant; more like being physically assaulted. He squirmed away from the coiling roots. They did not pursue him but continued to glide through the surrounding soil with playful abandon.

Grendel got to his feet and looked around, fearfully. Not being able to contemplate an opening to another plane of existence was one thing, but he was not sure that pedestrians would be able to so readily deny the presence of this monstrosity that did, at least, mimic natural conventions. He sprang to his feet and made to flee.

As he turned around, a voice, resonating with sighing of leaves, spoke. '*Still too much? I do forget how enclosed and limited the perceptions of this ecosphere's inhabitants are. Fine*, is this more to your liking?' With these last words, a drastic change had come over the voice. It sounded natural, almost human. *Almost*.

Grendel turned back round to face the tree, only to find that it had vanished. Instead, there stood large, bearded man. He was unnaturally tall and dressed in a biker's getup. He wore a leather jacket, torn at the arms that extended and bulged like great oak branches. Tattered black jeans covered his legs. His face was lost under a mop of willow leaf hair but his beard straggled down the length of his chin.

The person- no, Grendel had to remind himself- *the envoy*, gestured to a park bench nearby. 'Care to have seat with me, amigo?' the envoy asked in a gravelly voice.

'I guess not,' said Grendel, not knowing what else to say.

'Good call,' the bearded man said and trudged towards the worn bench. Grendel followed. The envoy took his seat. Grendel hesitated, and then sat himself down on the bench as far from the trans-dimensional ruffian as he could. 'Good, Grendel, good; you've taken your first step towards Omni- terrestrial enlightenment.'

'Or utter insanity,' Grendel interjected.

The envoy shrugged. 'Whatever works for you.'

'You know, for a being of incomprehensible power, you certainly like to speak in a colloquial manner.'

'Grendel, by entering this world, I've just assimilated all your people's languages and nuances. Let a wayward spirit have some fun.'

'Well, if you are with the equinox court then you must know why I've called you here.'

'You didn't *call* me here, Grendel. But as to your reasons, yes I know them. Yet thoughts and desires can be so rudimentary in their composition; why not put it into words. I am so enjoying this form of communication after all.'

Grendel couldn't decide whether this was supposed to be a test or part of the envoy's amusement. He'd best phrase this carefully, just in case. 'I, Grendel Juventino Hopper, magician, former student of the Universitatis Arcana, Oxford, wish to reach a beneficial accordance with the Equinox Court. To that end, I propose to offer a gift that is of the Court's own choosing, the significance of which may be repaid through a connection to their realm and access to its resources when I so desire.'

'In other words, you want us to give you some super magical mojo in exchange for a gift of *our* choice, seeing as how you were too lazy to think of one yourself.'

'How am I supposed to know what beings such as you would find valuable?' said Grendel, unable to mask the slight indignation from his voice.

'If you'd bothered to do a little further research, then you'd know that we of the Green Realm take great delight in devising games with you ephemeral beings. So here's what I'm gonna do for you, Grendel, I'm gonna give you access to the power of the *Enker-Green* right now. It's yours.'

'Really?!' spluttered Grendel.

'Yup, however, I'm gonna give you thirty-three hours. Thirty-three hours to learn how to harness and contain such power. If you haven't destroyed yourself by the end of that thirty-three hour period, then I'll be coming for you. And you better put on a good show for me when I do. Because if not, I'm gonna eat you, regurgitate you, shatter your soul, re-forge it into something more amusing, then eat you again and whatever else I can think of doing to you for the rest of forever... So do we have a deal?' He- *it*- held out a mud-caked hand that, Grendel could discern with mingled revulsion and yearning, was immersed in an aura of maliferous *green*.

Siren Knight

Arm's Length

Back when the ocean poured down your hands
Ochre nights spent formless
against your abandoned skin
I scratched you open and
licked at your ancient wounds

We clawed fractured flesh down to marrow
as my splintered nails tore at your barbed wire chest
Some days you'd laugh
and say I was aloof to my own allure
Then hold the Rizla onto
your broken tongue
And wet it like a litmus test

Now you clutch at my throat
and push your two salted fingers
in between
my scabbed words
the skin and the I
to pace your heartbeat with the dull strum of what's left
My mouth is blistered with acid burns again
And I wonder how something birthed so sudden
can take so long to die

Most of the time
I just remember how hard your heart was
beating in the car park of the train station
inside the aftermath
of our first kiss

Joe Legge

Tarrare

Professeur Percy approached a vomiting medical student outside the Hotel-Dieu Hospital and paused while the clean shaven young man wiped his mouth, inhaled deeply and looked up.

'Ca va?' Professeur Percy held out a handkerchief.

'Oui.' Came the response, breaths punctuated by globules of bile spat into the gutter. The medical student was facing the ground with his eyes squeezed shut.

'Tu avais vu Tarrare?'

The medical student looked up. Tarrare's presence here was held in the strictest confidence. But this man did not look like a criminal or one of the scandalmongers from le Mercure. In fact, he looked respectable in a fine suit of pistachio silk and carried with him a small leather bag, the kind the medical student had seen in expensive Paris boutiques and hoped to one day be able to afford.

'Oui,' the student said, 'il est dedans.' and pointed towards the hospital door.

Percy entered the building. He could have found the room with his eyes closed due to stench that hung in the air like fog. Every step caused an intensification of the reek which was coming from behind an unlocked door. Behind the door an autopsy was about to begin.

Before opening the door Percy took a moment to recall the Tarrare he had met four years prior; the pitiful freak who feared for his life was an odd creature, a medical anomaly, but no doubt human, although there was some debate.

A thick and invisible cloud hung like sour fumes from a witch's cauldron and enveloped the Professeur. He fixed his face in a blank expression and opened the door.

A grubby sheet covered a mound of flesh on a table in the centre of the room. Along the walls were bowls filled with smoking incense and tobacco. Percy presumed that the sheet had been clean before its placement and had absorbed grease, effluvia, and any other malodorous slime that eked out of the corpse. He wondered if the sheet had been put there as a gesture of respect for the dead. He suspected its true purpose was to hide from uninitiated eyes the distended and ghoulish corpse of the man whose death certificate named only as Tarrare, but whose obituary in Mercure de France called 'Tarrare the Depraved'.

He had been dead for less than a day yet the rotten stench and inflated body gave the appearance of a fortnight's decay. This rapid decomposition would no doubt be one of the objects of the autopsy but the primary goal was to ascertain an understanding of the man's inner workings - something that, in his life, no doctor or priest was ever able to explain and no amount of speculation or guesswork on their parts came close a cure. This consistent failure of reason gave rise to rumours among the unlearned that Tarrare had been cursed. That was that, in the opinion of the thieves and whores with whom Tarrare found pity, and there was no sense in questioning further.

Oddly, this mystical diagnosis satisfied him, not physically - nothing could - but he subsequently spent more than a year untroubled by the origin of his unyielding hunger and felt no burden of responsibility to find himself a cure. He merely went about his days searching for food wherever he might find it. Wrestling it out of the teeth of stray dogs, pilfered from market stalls, and in the garbage of butchers, bakers, and fishmongers who coined the name 'le Depreve'.

Percy, like most of the staff at the Soultz-Haut-Rhin Military Hospital had heard tales of Tarrare's almost unbelievable displays of appetite. They increased in absurdity from the swallowing of whole apples to the consumption of live cats. Percy was redressing a minor wound on the leg of a soldier on the day he first saw Tarrare. As he bandaged the soldier the young man repeated rumours that had been circulating about the man-beast who was kept apart from all others.

'...and then he regurgitated the fur and bones!' the Private said.

'Surely not.' Percy had said.

'I swear it, and there's more.' the Private said.

'Oh yes?' I suppose he ate his own legs or some such ridiculous thing.'

'Sir, no. But he's being exhibited tonight in the main hall.'

Percy cared little for the circus-like spectacle of the event and prided himself that his medical interest was driven, not only by his desire to increase in his scientific knowledge, but also by his humanist instincts and compassion for his fellow man, the same driving forces that had led him to medicine in the first place. However well intended he may have been, he failed to hide the stunned expression on his face as the event came to its denouement and he saw 'Tarrare The Depraved' in all his lack of glory.

Tarrare sat on a milking stool at the edge of a small wooden stage. Dr. Courville was speaking as Percy arrived and thrust himself onto his toes to better see the exhibit's face with its cheeks hanging loose and reaching the sides of his neck as though he were dressed in skin two sizes too large. Aside from this, and his unusually sunken eyes, he looked no different from any man one might pass in the street. Slightly scrawny, he hunched in his seat, staring at nothing as Dr. Courville concluded his talk.

'For the volunteer's willingness to participate, and to assuage any doubts that may still remain, we have provided for him some meat. Fourteen kilograms of lungs and liver from bulls, which we now invite him to eat.'

From the left of the stage a wheelbarrow was rolled on and

Tarrare raised his head while members of the audience withdrew from the smell and the sight of flies amassing on the livid mass of raw meat. Tarrare's jaw started to work as though already chewing and his eyes became more focussed.

Tarrare stood on his skinny legs, the uniform he had been given was ill fitting, the shirt flowed about his torso like a cape as he walked toward the barrow ignoring all who observed. Those who were nearest him could see the glisten of saliva wetting his lips and his nostrils appeared to flare wider with every inhalation. In the few seconds it had taken him to approach the meat he had taken to shivering and chewing the air. Spastic and random, his fingers twitched as drool slopped from his mouth and left dark patterns on his uniform.

He lunged for the meat, tearing chunks of it away from the total mass and gulping them down like it were an antidote he had long sought for. The speed of his consumption was limited only by the pace at which his arms could carry the offal from the wheelbarrow to his lips. His gullet offered no impediment, visibly widening to accommodate its task. The soldiers witnessing this grimaced at the sight: strips of pink meat sticking to The Monster's chin as blood drained from his hands to his elbows drenching his forearms entirely and soaking in to the rolled up sleeves of his shirt. The audience gasped when Tarrare fell to his knees. For a brief moment they believed him dead, his body refusing to acquiesce to the punishment forced upon it but Tarrare had dropped on purpose so that he could bend his back and neck into the barrow and bypass the use of his hands which were now too slippery to be of use. The depraved man swallowed great mounds of meat, his dark yellow teeth bit pieces away from the main load but were never used to chew. He sucked air in through his nose and with it came any liquids near his nostrils. The blood, a milky fluid from the lungs, oil and Tarrare's own sweat were swept inside his face with a loud rattling sound that was concluded with him hocking the mixture into his throat and drinking it down with as much gusto as he had shown while devouring the rest of the meal.

Percy was as still as though he had been frozen in ice. Never had his eyes seen a marvel as astounding and bizarre as this. He was almost knocked off his feet by the soldiers in front of him backing away from the monstrous display of hunger. Rather than retreat with them Percy worked through them until he was close enough to see wisps of vapour rising from Tarrare in such quantity as to flow through his clothes. And when he raised his head to more effectively suck down another bloody lump a cloud puffed up with his motion and dissipated about him. A second later the vapour reached Percy who was thrown immediately into coughing spasms and he bent double expecting to vomit, but knowing that to do so in front of Dr. Courville would mean being denied permission to study and treat the man on the stage. He forced himself to stand tall as the others in the congregation backed away and left the hall.

Tarrare was sitting on the stage with the wheelbarrow between his legs. His neck was still contorted so as to get his lips as close to his food as possible. From Percy's perspective he looked like a drunkard relieving himself of his drink. When he was gulping down nothing but air Tarrare stood and sucked the blood from his arms and hands before it dried. Percy's eyes widened, not at the barbaric display of behaviour but at the extraordinary phenomenon of biology he was witnessing. As Tarrare was now upright it was possible to see his full form once again and in the brief time since he had begun to gorge himself his stomach had grown immensely. His gut bulged out and stretched him so that his once billowing uniform was now a snug fit around this suddenly chubby man. The vapour had entirely drifted away but the rancid milk stench lingered thinly in the air. Dr. Courville returned to the stage and addressed the now almost empty room. His own face was pale and his forehead shined with perspiration. He stood away from Tarrare, turned to the room, and to the dismay of Professeur Percy's curiosity, he said only 'Dismissed,' before leaving the stage and pressing a handkerchief to his forehead.

Derek Littlewood

Trans-Siberian Journey

Within the museum,
an articulated wolf pricks
her ears anticipating Siberia;
to rattles of the shaman's drum,
her muzzle lifts in the sharp
stink of reindeer piss.
Potent with fly agaric
which he must drink
wafting across the tundra
to dream between worlds,
accompanied by howls & joiks.
The wolf stalks her quarry
towards Baba Yaga's hut
perched on chicken feet
scuttling over permafrost.
Where the witch-magic begins.

Dreams of Lake Baikal,
the hut, the stove,
strings of dried mushrooms:
outside larches against
vast whiteness.
A soft falling
of goose feathers
through time.

Masha, the baby mammoth
unearthed from permafrost
will not now be exhibited.
Each indigenous language
murmured in my ear
as precious as Masha,
as succulent as hazel-hen.
Khanty, Marian, Buryat
Kazakh, Koryak, Yakuk
Khakassan, Selkup, Tatr
Chuukese, Komi-Zyrian
Each echo and dissolve,
a thickening of the light
through the frost-ferns
of this vodka glass.

Joel Rawlin

Whispers

'Dad wouldn't want us in here.' A young girl's messy blond hair quivered as she whispered to her porcelain doll. She walked through an open door and further into the bedroom, lit by a slither of blue moonlight which shone through a gap in the curtains.

'Well I'm scared he'll find out.' She held the doll to her ear as if it spoke to her. 'Okay, well I do want to know what's in here.'

A clock's tick – tick – tick was subdued by the heavy breathing of Megan Williams in deep sleep. Her white bedsheets lay lose on top of her fidgeting body. Her dyed black hair was wet and matted. She turned over as the girl edged closer to the bed.

'I just want to see what's underneath.' The girl lowered the doll and pulled back the duvet. Megan lay bare; her arms were dotted with scars, some still red raw. She shivered. Her breath formed a light mist.

The girl tugged at the covers until they lay in a heap on the floor. Megan fidgeted in her sleep; her subconscious searching for warmth.

Wild laughter echoed through the house. The girl stood silent as she held onto the doll and looked about the room. Nowhere to hide.

'What are you doing out of bed?' A voice, just as haunting and malevolent as the laughter. The girl squeezed the doll close to her chest and ran for the bedroom door. It slammed behind her.

Megan jolted awake, her breath was still a light grey cloud. She leant over to the bedside cabinet and switched on a lamp, its yellow light cast shadows up the walls. They were motionless, stagnant even, just waiting for their creator to move or to be consigned back into darkness.

Megan glanced around the room. Her eyes darting to every threatening silhouette, then they lingered on the door. Shut. Not as she'd left it.

The curtains fluttered and through the gap Megan saw that the window was wide open. After another look around the room she rubbed her eyes and sat up. The clock read 3:48.

She clambered out of bed and gathered the bedsheets, knocking over an empty bottle of wine as she did so. She then pulled the window to and closed the latch before slumping back down onto the bed.

'Get a grip' Megan thought to herself as she wrapped the covers around her. She looked over toward an unopened box of tablets on the bedside cabinet and considered them before switching off the light and turning her back to the pills.

***

A ray of sunlight broke through the curtains and onto the bed where Megan was cocooned within her duvet. Her phone vibrated against the wooden cabinet beside her. She stirred in her sleep, turned over and opened her eyes. She reached toward the phone, picked it up and read the caller I.D, Anna Williams.

'Hell – Hello.' Megan's voice was raspy and dry.

'Hey Sis!' Anna was chirpy and loud. 'I didn't wake you, did I?'

'No, no. It's fine. I've been up a while.' She looked up at the clock. 11:20. Anna laughed.

'Liar! I know when you've slept in.' She continued to talk and Megan barely listened only concentrating on regaining full consciousness. 'Megan – Megan? Are you okay?' There was genuine concern in her voice.

'I'm fine, I just had a bad night. What did you want anyway?' Megan's voice croaked as she spoke.

'Lunch? I thought we could meet at the pub around two?'

'Yeah, sure. I'll just get ready. See you soon, okay?' After saying their goodbyes Megan hung up. She threw the phone onto her bed, yawned, stretched and headed into the bathroom.

* * *

Megan could feel a cool breeze as she stepped from the train and onto the concrete platform. A metal fence hugged the perimeter. It contained the deserted platform and shut out a thick woodland that surrounded the station.

She pulled a jacket off and wrapped it around her waist. The pub was only a short walk from the station but the heat would make it a struggle. Why Anna had to pick this pub was beyond Megan. It was nice inside but it was rural and the area creeped her out.

The station was unstaffed and unloved. Paint peeled off a wooden shack which had a hand painted sign above it, *Pluckley Station Ticket Office*. Its windows were cracked and the door hung at an angle off its hinges. She walked toward the door and pushed it. Locked. Just as she suspected. She let out a frustrated sigh and looked for another exit.

The only signs of life were from birds who chirped in the trees. A cluster of dead leaves rustled slowly along the platform and onto the track. Megan walked toward a putrid green gate. As she got closer the wind picked up. The gentle breezes converted into strong explosions of wind. The trees were blown about, as if being shaken and strangled by the wind's clasp. Dying leaves flew from their branches and joined with the tree's shadows as they crept toward Megan with each gale.

The birds no longer chirped. Their silence chilled Megan as it wrapped itself around her body, weighing her down. She stood rigid and stared directly into the trees.

There was something there in the woods. A black silhouette of a man, cast onto the trunk of a tree. Megan was immobilised by the obscure figure. There was nothing in the woods to create it.

She continued to stare intently at it, willing it to move. To show her it was real. To do something other than just watch her.

The silence was broken by a whisper, carried in the wind. A soft voice, a child's voice. T*ime – to – play*. Goose-bumps covered Megan's scarred arms as the whisper was followed by footsteps along the platform behind her. She couldn't move though. Couldn't turn to see who *or what* inched toward her. With each step Megan's chest thumped, her heart was attempting its final escape.

And then... nothing.

Megan felt like she'd been thawed out by the autumn sun, the cold that had captured her had vanished, as did the strong winds. She turned on the spot and looked up the platform. Empty. She then scanned the trees. Again... nothing. She was alone on the platform, joined only by the chirping of hidden birds.

* * *

The pub resembled an old manor house built from bulky grey stones. Ivy rose up the walls and decorated it with patches of green. The interior was modern yet lost none of the history with thick wooden beams that connected to the low ceiling. The bar was spacious and had a restaurant attached through a doorway.

Megan and Anna sat on a soft brown leather couch by the fireplace. The flames hissed and crackled as they burnt through thick logs. They both held glasses of red wine, each took sips as the other spoke.

'It was just a bad dream but it felt so real, like that girl were really in my room.' Megan placed the glass down on a wooden table by her legs and looked up at Anna who frowned.

'Is this the first time it's happened?' Anna replied, she was curious but disbelieving.

'Well, I've had the nightmares before. But it's the first time I've woken up feeling like something was in my room'

'You have been okay, haven't you?' Anna watched as Megan

stared beyond her and out the window. 'Megan? What are you looking at?' Anna turned herself around and looked outside. Satisfied there was nothing there, she twisted back.

'Yeah, yeah sorry. I'm fine.' Megan was focused back on Anna, she forced a smile.

'And the girl? Did you recognise her?' Anna asked cautiously.

'No, I didn't see her face. I just know she was carrying a doll. Like the doll I used to have before...' She paused. 'It's nothing though, just a bad dream. It just felt so real.'

* * *

The kitchen sink was filled with grimy water. An irregular drip hit the stagnated pool, it rippled through the reflection of the moon. Plates were left on the counter – food residual left to rot.

The occasional crack of thunder and flash of lightening would cause Megan to flinch as she stood over the sink wearing bright yellow latex gloves. She would prove to Anna that she was fine and a clean house would help. Megan picked a plate up from the counter and began to wash. She scrubbed the dirt off and hummed along to soft acoustic music that was playing from a radio in the living room. The song was subdued by rain that tap-tap-tapped away at the window in front of Megan; but from what she could make out she'd enjoyed. It was the first bit of peace she'd had in a while, Megan had thought.

As she finished washing the final dish the radio station began to move in and out of signal. Then it settled on a deafening blast of static. Megan hurried into the living room. The radio was sat on a display shelf next to a picture of Megan and Anna as children. They were hugging; their blond hair was captured blowing in the wind. Megan picked up the radio and after re-tuning with no luck she switched it off and returned to the kitchen.

Without the music Megan could hear the kitchen clock more clearly. Every monotonous tick- tick- tick put her more on edge. She glanced about her, small beads of sweat trickled down her forehead. The ticking seemed to get louder; it was as if each passing second was attempting to outdo the one before it.

Her hands shook, but she wasn't nervous and the sun's warmth hugged her skin. She walked over to a cupboard and removed a wine glass. She filled it to the brim and drank half the glass. Yet she continued to shake. Only now the sun was hidden behind some clouds and the cold's icy nails scratched at her skin.

A distorted reflection in the window puzzled her. Then it moved into clear view. A man, but it couldn't be. Her Father. Her insides clenched up and she lurched over, dropping her glass. It shattered, leaving a trail of crystal specks in a sticky red puddle.

'No, no. You're not here. You're not real'. Megan trembled and watched the reflection; it was standing and staring at the back of her. She spun around. Behind her was just an empty hallway. Megan screamed and threw all the recently washed items off the side. They smashed upon impact, china and glass fragments carpeted the floor.

'WHO ARE YOU? WHAT DO YOU WANT?' She shouted at the emptiness, tears slid down her cheeks and she fell into a heap amongst the broken objects.

Megan sat like this for a while, her hands, cut and bleeding. She left red stains on her face as she wiped her eyes. She rocked herself to the beat of the clock, its tedious rhythm the only sound in the house; until... swish – creak, swish – creak, swish – creak.

Megan jumped up and looked toward the sounds. Outside, a girl swung back and forth on a homemade wooden swing attached to an oak tree. She held a doll in her arms and smiled up at Megan. There was something about that doll that held Megan's gaze. She'd recognised it, but not just from her dreams.

'No, no. You are only a fucking nightmare!'

Megan ran out into the garden and into the rain, leaving the kitchen door to be slammed shut. She walked toward the swing.

It swung back and forth, but the girl and her doll were gone, the garden was empty.

***

Megan sat against the bedroom door. Her mobile held to her ear.

'I'm telling you it was the same girl from my dream. I know what I saw.' Her voice whimpered as tears stained her red cheeks.

'Okay, okay. I believe you. Was there anybody else?' Anna spoke softly. An attempt to calm the situation.

'Dad. I saw Dad...' There was an eerie silence.

'You know he's dead Megs. We – we saw it happen. You remember, don't you?'

'Of course I remember. He tried to fucking kill me.' More tears streamed down Megan's face. She rocked back and forth, knocking her head against the door.

'I know – I'm...'

'He killed mum and then he went after me. He called me an abomination and laughed as he hit me, as he took a knife and pierced the eyes of my doll.' Megan rocked back and forth.

'I know' Anna sobbed through a crackling signal.

'Laughing as he said he would replace my eyes with the dolls. Saying the black eyes would suit me better. Megan's eyes were black and glossy, she continued to rock.

'STOP. Just stop. I know what he did and I don't need reminding!'

'He's coming for me. He always said he'd get me in the end.' Megan threw the phone against the wall. It cracked and shattered, breaking apart on impact.

***

There was a knock at the door then a key was inserted, turned and the door unlocked. It was pushed open allowing a stream of light into the room.

Megan was sitting cross legged underneath the mahogany

display cabinet. She clasped onto a butcher's knife and rocked, gently knocking the cabinet with her head.

She looked up as Anna entered but continued to chant, *'I can hear you speaking'* on loop. Anna hurried over to her side and leant out to touch her.

'NO. Stop moving and be quiet.' Megan stared at Anna, 'Can't you hear them?'

'Hear what? It's silent.'

'Silent?' Megan was puzzled. 'They are speaking all around you'

'There is no-one here Megan, only me.'

'Can't you hear the whispers from the dead lips of the dolls? All the dolls, they are watching us. Daddy got me one and then he killed it and now it watches me.'

Anna switched on a lamp. A flood of yellow engulfed the room, Megan screamed as if the light had burnt her. She was staring at Anna, but her stare was different, wrong. Her eyes were black and lifeless, like a doll's eyes.

Megan stood and held the knife out. She was ready to attack. She stared not at Anna, but behind her. At a figure shrouded in darkness.

Megan lurched forward and pushed her knife toward the shadow, toward Anna. It slid effortlessly into her throat. She fell to her knees and coughed up blood onto the carpet until with each breath she swallowed and choked more.

The figure was gone. Megan stood over Anna as her body convulsed. They were alone. Megan dropped the knife and backed away from her sister until her back slammed into the display cabinet knocking off the picture of the sister's embrace. Megan picked it up and fell to the ground. She held the picture to her chest and curled into a ball.

'Shhh... Anna. Stop talking now, you'll wake up dad.' Megan whispered.

Anna Lawrence Pietroni

'Night thickened and from the north, snowflakes'[1]

and from the south, the women flew in on the back of sparrows
and from the east, the gannet-ogres strode
and from the west, the broken-reeded sap-stripped soldiers
took shape in lost children, wandering bewildered by the road.
(Holed up, too warm; the shutters suck the marrow from
   the moonlight,
my son's curls damp and slick beneath my palm.
The waters pound The Mend below our window,
the seawall flung out in a crooked arm).
Ma, I heard that when the women had dismounted
The sparrows were spit-roasted without heads.
I heard they wore the sparrow-beaks as totems
And wove a noose from broken sparrow-legs.

The morning stalks us with wet feet and bitter sulphur breezes.
I've checked, Johnny. The Mend's intact. No breaches.

---

1 'The Seafarer', *The Earliest English Poems*, ed. Michael Alexander (London: Penguin, 1991)

David Roberts

The Petition

January 1709. Margaret, a distressed widow, writes to the Queen.

If Her Majesty would kindly consider the service done by her first husband Pemell, an officer in the wars against the Papists. How he had got together a band of men and taken on the French privateers, commandeering a mere fishing boat and storming them in their warship. Eight Papists had died, another fourteen wounded and captured. The French captain himself had been brought to Youghal and tried. Her Pemell was a fair-minded man, a man among men. He went through the French ship and divided the spoils fairly among his crew, with a portion to himself. How they celebrated. How they loved him.

Yes, that would be a good start.

The late King himself knew of Pemell's bravery. Was it the Lord Chancellor or the Lord Lieutenant who had told him of it? It was a Lord of Some Sorts, for sure. They had promised riches, but Death shut their coffers tight. Her Pemell was killed. She did not know how. They would not tell her, they said, because it would distress her so. You cannot distress me more, she replied. Then they did. They told her Pemell had been no officer, just an ordinary sergeant. But she would not bother the Queen with such trifles. After all, what officer could have conducted himself better?

It was a compounding of ill fortune. By some roguish trickery, Pemell had lost the best part of a fortune: a thousand pounds a year, she reckoned. Somehow it had seeped away, so she had supported him with what little she had, and her own money had gone the same way. Of his love of cards and good claret she said nothing. The Queen would not be interested in such stuff, surely. But their children – yes, there was their boy Samuel, who had gone away to sea and, as far as she knew, died in the service, for she had not heard from him these eighteen months. Samuel had done them proud. Her Majesty must know that.

And then she had married George. An Irish boy with a melancholy air and a wit like a cat's claw. Her Majesty had perhaps heard of George's writings and his way with words. He had first spoken to her through her mourning dress and she felt her veil lifting like dawn. It would have been the same for any woman, even the Queen herself, perhaps. But she would not write so.

For George she took to wearing her best dress and borrowed from friends so he would not think her poor. One day in a coach they passed a handsome lodging near the Exchange she permitted him to conclude was her father's house. He in turn spoke of his plays, his friends at the theatre, his benefit night earnings and his dealings with the prosperous men who printed his books; he thought his friend Bobby Wilks the actor the finest fellow in the world and his late father, a country parson burned out by the Papists, the unluckiest (then George, a boy of thirteen, had joined King William's army against the Papists, or so he said – that was one story she never believed). It was Bobby Wilks who first told him he should write and leave Dublin with him to go to London.

So George and Margaret fell into this way of picturing each others' fortunes and families, and how comfortable they would be together. And so they married, she and her George.

On their wedding night he had been as quick with his tongue as ever, in a manner that pleased her from head to toe and many ways between (no, she had better not tell that to the Queen). But the following morning he said he found himself short of cash for their breakfast, and asked if she had any. She could only look at her borrowed shoes. No, she said. She had nothing but what she was wearing. And even that was not hers. For days they said nothing. He would disappear of a sudden and, she thought, wander the streets. One day he told her he had been to Gravesend to watch the tide go out.

Yet he forgave her in time and she found it in herself to forgive him, as long as he found himself a living. Yes, she had said that to him. Find yourself a living, or if you will not, find yourself a fortune like a real man, like my late husband Pemell. And lose it again like he did, I suppose, George's sharp tongue spat. Then she did not see him for weeks.

He had said he was going to stay with Bobby Wilks, but she never found him there. When he returned, it was to tell her his new play had failed and, since she was so beloved of a soldier man, he was to join the army. Bobby had paid for him to gain a commission. Lieutenant Farquhar of the Earl of Orrery's Foot. Or was it the Duke of Ormond's Foot? She could not be sure. But she would write to them both in favour of her petition and they would attest to Lieutenant Farquhar's service. They would tell Her Majesty of his loyalty; how her beloved George had died in her service, in a manner of speaking at least.

He was no soldier like Pemell. No swaggering hero, just a recruiting officer. But he was, at least, a genuine officer. They sent him to the Midlands, to Shrewsbury and Lichfield, and he came back with stories of fine houses and taverns and lords and ladies and lads he had sent off to fight the Papists. And did you meet some fine girls in your travels, she asked him. He only laughed and joshed her for a jealous nag, but she saw in his eyes that he had.

His travels had saved him, he said. A new play appeared, and it brought him money. The life of a recruiting officer was merry stuff for a play. For once they ate well and bought new clothes. They even thought to find new lodgings. Then, one cold day in April when the spring flowers were nipped and their petals falling, his coughing began. Spit it out George, she had said, it is but a ticklish phlegm. But he could not stop nor speak to admonish her. Neither of them slept that night, and in the morning she saw blood on the sheet between them. Slowly, he grew pale and tired. He spent his days in bed. As for writing, he could barely lift his hand. No one came to visit, fearing his sickness.

Then one day, at last, Bobby Wilks the actor came round. With his brave Irish smile and a bearish hug Bobby Wilks took him in his arms and said George, George, what ails you? And George could only say he was dying and what were his poor family to do. Then Bobby said you must write, George. Write us another play. Write, cried George. I can hardly breathe, man. I cannot lift my hand to keep the sweat from my eyes, and you would have me write? Yes, said Bobby with his brave smile. Just write, damn you.

So then George roused himself and wrote. He spelled out the story with mist in his eyes, lying like the truth, as he called it. Two lads up from London, out of their fortunes and seeking an heiress. Bobby and George on their way from Ireland, ten years before. His thoughts dozed back to Lichfield, to a tavern and a fine house, to plotting Papists and maids waiting patiently in line for seduction. But his finest gift of a character was for Margaret. He called her Mrs Sullen: a lonely, desolate wife, stranded in the provinces, made bitter by her marriage, looking for the door out. George, she told him, that is not me, as she looked over the draft. I am your own Margaret, my dear. I would not leave you. Then he had swept the papers to the floor, thrown his head back and cried and wailed until the coughing returned and he could cry no more. The next day he was dead.

And so Margaret, a distressed widow, writes to the Queen. George had taught her – lying like the truth, he had called his writing as he lay dying. Why should not her pen do the same for the same promise of fine clothes and a good dinner nightly? She tells how Pemell, a fine officer, had sacked the French privateer and slain the entire crew, and how her boy Samuel had died in

Her Majesty's service. Why, her late husband George had also been a soldier, the son of an eminent divine of the Church in Ireland burned out of his fortune by the Papists. As a mere boy, George had gone to war with King William. He had served in the army and seen action at Valencia and Monjuic. He had died nobly in Her Majesty's service.

Your Majesty, she writes, help a poor army widow in her distress.

Derek Littlewood

The Secret Languages of Ireland

Breaking camp,
they left at dawn
without waking a soul
their wagons consigned
to flames.
              Anna na mBreag

Veronica swirled *poitín* against the light;
cautioned me not to smash my teeth
with the bottle as we swigged.
As I felt her Irish tongue
in my mouth, I pondered
that the back slang for kiss from Irish *póg* becomes *gop*

in the cant. Thirty years on
in this seminar room we teased apart the place-lore
of Friel's *Translations*; smelt turf
cut with a loy. Eamon from Co. Clare and myself,
the Englishman, who named his son Ronan.
The Irish for little seal.

At interview Ashling asked eventually
if she would need to declare officially
she'd had a child out of wedlock
over the water. She spoke some *Gaeilge*,
but had not the book learning. They
had sent her out of school early.

In class she recited *Mise Raifteirí an file*
by heart with an aside that the nuns
equally patriotic and religious
would slash her knuckles with a ruler
if she stumbled. Outside in the English
Midlands it was a soft day.

Nostos - a sweet sickness for home.
Bitter dregs from a chipped cup.
Sweating from a Smethwick foundry,
Seán unwrapped a knock-off death mask
of James Joyce. In aluminium, not bronze –
still a steal at a hundred pounds. He was

narked neither Eamon nor myself
wanted the thing mute on our wall.
That building where we taught
will be pulled down next year,
already over the rubble the blackbird's
song echoes from Lough Derg.

Rhoda Greaves

Her Body

It started with her left lung. Three weeks later her right one went the same way.

'It's like when we used to bake hula-hoop packets and make them into those shrivelled badges.' That's how she described it.

'How come you're still breathing then?'

'I'm not,' she said, placing my palm between her sweaty breasts.

Next it was her colon: 'How do you take a shit?' I asked.

'I don't,' she told me, but I'd smelt her farts.

Her liver packed up. Her toenails peeled away, and, one-by-one, her fingers loosened at the sockets: when I tried to hold her hand it fell away from my grip. Her bones grew holes. Next it was her pancreas.

'It's okay,' she said, force-feeding herself Snickers.

She stunk like rotten meat and sugar, so I held my breath when we kissed.

Before too long she was packing up and moving to the cemetery.

'Shall I bring a sleeping bag?' This would be my first time at her new place.

'No need,' she said, her eye leaking smoke from a borrowed cigarette.

We stayed up most of the night putting on posh accents and downing jägerbombs with the ghosts. And when I unhooked my body from her corpse the next morning, I felt a sharp crack at the centre of my ribcage. I stood up to leave her and heard a long slow hiss.

Notes on the Contributors

Jan Barker

Jan Barker lives in Birmingham and is studying for an MA in Creative Writing at Birmingham City University. She is pursuing her interest in short fiction and drama following an early exit from a career in Human Resources. Jan is drawn to the themes of outsiders and the slightly peculiar, and cites Shirley Jackson, Neil Gaiman and Zenna Henderson as influences.

Ted Bonham

Ted Bonham is James Horrocks, the 5,122,808,515th person alive on Earth and 80,093,634,401st person to have lived since history began. He is a PhD Researcher in English (Creative Writing) at Birmingham City University where he is working on Ted's autobiography *Notes to Self*. Bio writing is not his forte.

Jim Crace

Jim Crace is an award winning writer and well respected alumnus from Birmingham College of Commerce (now part of Birmingham City University.) His novel *Quarantine*, won the Whitbread Novel award and was shortlisted for the Man Booker Prize as was his latest novel *Harvest*, which also won the International Impac Dublin Literary Award.

Nicholas Doran

Nicholas Doran has always been intrigued by the creation of imaginary worlds and the ways in which they inspire creativity in others. He is currently completing an MA in Creative Writing at Birmingham City University and specializes in quirky, speculative fiction. He hopes to one day become a published novelist and a writer for Tabletop Roleplaying Games.

Rhoda Greaves

Rhoda Greaves is a Visiting Lecturer and PhD Creative Writing student at Birmingham City University, and is also an Associate Editor at Short Fiction magazine. Her stories have been commended or listed in several prizes including the Bridport Short Story Prize, Manchester Fiction Prize and Aesthetica Creative Writing Award, and her work has been published in a variety of literary magazines.

Helena Hoar

An MA student taking writing seriously at long last. While at BCU has won prizes for Creative Non-fiction and Reading into Writing, as well as the Dean's Award, and has been commended in the Orwell Society's dystopian fiction competition. Usually writes short stories, but excited to be writing a novel about a real Black Country murder.

Olivia Hodgson

Olivia was born in 1995 and grew up in Birmingham. She is currently completing her final year studying English and Creative Writing at Birmingham City University. She volunteers as a theatre technician and listens to too much Morrissey.

Tony Howe

Dr Anthony Howe hails from the North East of England and went to University in Liverpool; he has taught at both bits of Oxbridge. He iscurrently Reader in English Literature at Birmingham City University and lives in Arle, Cheltenham. He doesn't write much poetry.

Richard Hughes

Richard Hughes has recently completed his BA at Birmingham City University where he was on the English and Creative Writing route way. He is now working as a Research Administrator at the Jubilee Centre for Character & Virtues. He is both a writer and musician.

Siren Knight

If you should seek her out, Siren Knight is often to be found in coffee shops or libraries with ink stained fingers and paint in her hair. She was awarded a commendation from the 'Orwell society' for her short story 'Slaves to the Transition' in 2015 and is currently studying a Master's degree in writing. 'Noir' was first published in Siren call's (no affiliation) e-zine 'Supernatural' under the title 'Recurring Darkness' 2015.

Gregory Leadbetter

Gregory Leadbetter's poetry collections include *The Fetch* (Nine Arches Press, 2016) and the pamphlet *The Body in the Well* (Happenstance, 2007). His book *Coleridge and the Daemonic Imagination* (Palgrave Macmillan, 2011) won the University English (formerly CCUE) Book Prize 2012. He is Reader in Literature and Creative Writing, and Director of both the MA in Creative Writing and the Institute Creative and Critical Writing at Birmingham City University.

Derek Littlewood

Derek Littlewood teaches Writing Poetry and Nature Writing in the School of English, Birmingham City University. He was longlisted in 2015 National Poetry Competition. He lives in Worcestershire with his family and is a keen amateur naturalist.

Shirley Lloyd

Shirley Lloyd is studying for an MA in Creative Writing. She is exploring her interests in fiction, stage and radio drama writing. She is interested in the theme of relationships, in particular their similarities and differences as determined by cultural, social and economic circumstances. She admires the works of Maya Angelou, Alice Walker and Andrea Levy.

Chuck Newsey

Chuck Newsey is from Chicago, IL and currently lives in Birmingham, UK. Chuck is a writer and enjoys the beautiful and the strange. She has been in bands, worked in offices, factories, and record stores. She has been the hero, the victim, the confidant, the liar and was homeless for a time. She has an Undergraduate and Masters Degree from Birmingham City University. One day, Chuck hopes to race a tumbleweed.
Chucknewsey.blogspot.co.uk

Anna Lawrence Pietroni

Anna Lawrence writes poetry and prose and is beginning to write audio drama. Her first novel, *Ruby's Spoon*, was published by Chatto & Windus in 2010. She is particularly interested in exploring, through writing, the interaction of the magical and the industrial, the role of architecture in shaping community (whether it's prisons or convents) and women's medieval spirituality.

Joel Rawlin

Joel Rawlin is a writer of short stories, novels and screenplays. He grew up on the Romney Marsh in Kent where he developed a keen interest in horror/ghost stories as well as action, thrillers and comedies. He moved up to Birmingham in 2012, not only for his love of all things Aston Villa but to study a BA in English Literature and an MA in Creative Writing.

David Roberts

David Roberts is Pro Vice Chancellor and Dean of the Faculty of Arts, Design and Media at Birmingham City University. He is currently working on his thirteenth book, a biography of the Irish dramatist George Farquhar. Recent titles include Restoration Plays and Players (Cambridge University Press, 2014) and Games for English Literature (with Izabela Hopkins, Libri Publishing, 2016). He has also published a novel, The Life of Harris the Actor, and writes programme essays for the Royal Opera House.

Jack Roberts

Jack is an English and Creative Writing student from Rugby who watches way too many television dramas. This might not be such a bad thing, as he wants to write for TV. He enjoys writing short fiction and scripts, and works best when listening to David Bowie.

Jack Warren

Jack Warren was raised in the West Country and his work has appeared both online & in print. In autumn of 2015 he spent three weeks hiking along the River Severn, sleeping in fields, flood banks & angler's hides. The poems featured here form part of a larger work about the journey.

Dan Witherall

Dan Witherall has seen three short films produced and played at festivals, and a showreel directed by BAFTA-winner Michael B. Clifford. Currently, he is a script editor on an upcoming feature starring veteran actor David Warner. He is also the co-writer and executive producer of a U.S. feature film that is awaiting acceptance from festivals worldwide. His Twitter account is very NSFW: @TheWitherall.